D0775492

UNTAMED SPIRIT

AROUND THE WORLD
ON A MOTORCYCLE

DORIS MARON

iUniverse, Inc.
New York Bloomington

Untamed Spirit
Around the World on a Motorcycle

iUniverse books may be ordered through booksellers or by contacting:

iUniverse
1663 Liberty Drive
Bloomington, IN 47403
www.iuniverse.com
1-800-Authors (1-800-288-4677)

Because of the dynamic nature of the Internet, any Web addresses or links contained in this book may have changed since publication and may no longer be valid. The views expressed in this work are solely those of the author and do not necessarily reflect the views of the publisher, and the publisher hereby disclaims any responsibility for them.

ISBN: 978-1-4502-2851-0 (sc)
ISBN: 978-1-4502-2852-7 (ebook)

Printed in the United States of America

iUniverse rev. date: 05/17/2010

Contents

FOREWORD

I was there on that rainy summer day in Emily Murphy Park on the Edmonton (Alberta) riverbank, when friends said goodbye and "Good Luck" to Doris Maron.

Many of us envied her; none of us would be brave enough or determined enough to undertake an adventure of this magnitude.

In the following three years she rode her "Magna" through forty-three countries on six continents, covering over 120,000 kilometers.

There were difficulties posed by weather, bad roads, pro-bureaucratic border crossings and sometimes, bad water and food. But the overriding impression Doris returned with, was, that ordinary people all over the world are wonderfully friendly and helpful. Fellow adventurers she met along the way, whether on motorcycles, bicycles or on foot, were all cut out of the same cloth.

This strong woman, riding all alone, found the way to get to know the "real world", something you can never do by flying to all the tourist hot spots around the globe.

Reading this book will help you to understand.

Rudi Zacsko Sr.

ACKNOWLEDGMENTS

Many people have encouraged me to write about my experiences traveling as a single female around the globe. The list is unending and I thank each and every one of you.

The first person I must thank is Colleen McFarland. Colleen was my biggest supporter when I was planning my journey and her support continued throughout my travels. Colleen, you cannot imagine how much your e-mails meant to me when I was alone in foreign countries— Thank you. Thank you to Rudi Zacsko Sr. for writing the foreword for my book and for all the friendly advice about places previously traveled on your motorcycling journeys. Thank you to the staff at iUniverse for your recommendations and patience.

Thank you to all my friends in the motorcycling community who encouraged me to write and helped build my confidence. Thank you to all my friends outside of the motorcycling community for your support and interest in my story. Last but not least, thank you to my family for standing by me and for not writing me off as a *vagabond*. A special *thanks* goes to my sister Florence for always being there in my times of need—you are a true friend.

I wish to say a very special thanks to all the wonderful people I met during my travels; those who were so gracious with their hospitality, those I traveled with briefly, those who helped me in so many ways, and those who were just there to add to my experiences.

Thank you.

Introduction

My dream was to travel around the world

I cannot tell you where the dream came from or when it began, but it seems it has been with me forever. In 1989, at the age of forty-one I learned how to ride a motorcycle and that was the beginning of my travels in North America. Each summer from 1990 onward I did a two- to four-week trip on my bike. By the end of year 2000 I had traveled in forty-one states of America and all ten provinces in Canada. North America is a wonderful place to travel with landscapes so diverse and spectacular one can never tire of its beauty. I just could not seem to get enough. Everywhere I went people were wonderful and I felt perfectly safe. Up to this point most of my travels were with other people— sometimes one friend, other times a group of friends, and many times family members who ride motorcycle.

The more places I discovered the more my thoughts about traveling around the world grew. Every time I thought seriously about doing it, old anxieties would surface—I can't do this alone, I don't have enough money, what if I have trouble with my bike, I'll miss my children and grandchildren. So many excuses kept rolling through my mind.

To make matters worse, many well meaning friends and family members tried to discourage me. They expressed their fears of going out into the unknown world alone. They repeated horror stories they had heard somewhere. I am sure they were genuinely concerned about me, but as I listened to their tales, my own anxieties grew. Then one day I realized that most of their stories were from second hand information and not their own experiences. I could not, and *would* not allow them to impose their fears upon me.

In the summer of year 2000 I traveled across Canada and the United States from coast to coast with two other motorcycling enthusiasts. We traveled for seven weeks crossing the United States from the Pacific Ocean to the Atlantic, then back across Canada from the Atlantic to the Pacific. I enjoyed the adventure so much I hated to see it come to an end. I began to wonder what it would be like to travel without a time frame, without a schedule, and ride around the globe.

"Thoughts are seeds that, if fed and watered, grow into realities."

I fed and watered my seeds daily. I laminated a map of the world and put it in the center of my kitchen table. Every time I sat down to eat, it would be right there in front of me. I drew potential routes with a washable pen, enjoying the dream. I am sure I changed the lines on it every day as I read about places I wanted to see. With each new day my dream became more of a reality. I believe we create our own destiny—that, God, the Divine Spirit of the Universe, has given us the tools to make our life whatever we desire it to be.

It happened one day towards the end of year 2000; I made the decision to *"just do it!"* All the fears I had—I can't travel alone, the world is too dangerous, I don't have enough money—came flooding in. Then it hit me! These fears will always be there. I am fifty-two years old and if I wait for everything to be perfect, I'll soon be too old to go. At that moment I asked myself a crucial question. "Doris, what would be your biggest regret if you knew you were to die tomorrow?"

The answer came without hesitation and without doubt. "My biggest regret would be that I never embraced the opportunity to see the rest of the world."

In that instant my decision was made!

A miraculous thing happens when one *"decides."* I remember only parts of a verse I had taped to my refrigerator door. It goes like this: *"The moment one is committed, Providence moves too. Doors open where there were no doors before. All sorts of things occur to help one that would otherwise never have occurred."* There is more, but these are the words that spring from my memory.

With the decision final, I had a lot of business to take care of. One of the biggest tasks was to find a good financial advisor to take over my client base. Most of my clients had become good friends and some were family. I cared about each and every one of them and wanted to make sure that they would be happy with a new advisor. I would not turn them over to just anyone. The person I chose to approach was very much like myself and I was thrilled when she accepted my proposal. That completed a very important piece to my plan.

The next big issue was my rental property. My tenants were with me for a lot of years and I could not bring myself to sell while they lived there. Then, without expecting it, one of my tenants gave notice to leave. I took that as another sign. I renovated that side of the duplex and decided to list it for sale by owner. If I could sell it on my own while it was empty, I would let it go. In the month that I renovated, I had two offers. One offer was to buy the whole duplex and keep the tenants in the other side. I could not believe my luck—or was it luck? Maybe it was the Divine Power of the universe taking care of business. Whatever you choose to believe is up to you. I knew that this was another step towards my goal.

I had to get my immunization shots, check out travel and health insurance, motorcycle insurance, dispose of my personal belongings, build a Web site and spend as much time as possible with my children and grandchildren. The biggest decision of all was to decide what motorcycle to take.

I was set on taking my 1997, candy apple red Goldwing; but my biking friends suggested that was not a good idea. This is a very big bike, would cost a lot to ship, and could become a problem in some countries where bikes of this size are seldom seen. Thus, I started my search. Everyone has their favorites and friends tried to persuade me to buy what they thought was best. It was a difficult decision. I looked at and test rode several different makes and models. Then one day I test rode a 750cc Honda magna. It was instant love. The bike felt good, handled well, had lots of power and really looked sharp. Most important of all, it is known for its reliability. After a couple of test rides, I knew this was the one. I purchased the magna and, with much sorrow, sold my Goldwing. That beautiful red bike and I had been riding companions for four years, and together we had logged almost one hundred thousand kilometers. It was hard to let her go.

I began spreading the word around within the motorcycle clubs in Edmonton, in hopes that someone would join me on this trip. I sent an e-mail to the head chapter of Women in the Wind in the United

States in hopes that one of my *Sisters* of Women in the Wind would join me. I also started making inquiries about sponsorship for my trip. Maybe I could get some funding by advertising for motorcycle related companies or writing articles for magazines.

I contacted several motorbike companies and magazines as well as motorbike clothing companies. Weeks would pass without any answers. Follow-up phone calls produced rejections. Some of the bike companies turned me down flat right from the first inquiry. I had my hopes up with one motorcycle magazine and a clothing company, but in the end neither one came through. I did not persist with this line of finance, even though many of my friends suggested that it should be easy to get sponsorship. The idea of a female traveling solo around the world on a motorcycle sounds like a good story. I thought so too, but it was not meant to be. I would have to fund this myself. I expect the people I contacted thought my plan was impossible and that I would never complete such a journey.

In the mean time, I started the immunization program. There were a lot of shots to get and both arms felt like pincushions after awhile. I was certainly glad when they were complete. Inquiring about health and travel insurance was interesting. I discovered it was not so easy to get when you plan on being out of the country for more than a year. I finally bought coverage for the year and decided to face the issue of renewal when the time came. Insurance for my motorcycle was even more difficult. I could not find a company in Canada that would insure me outside of North America. The company I regularly dealt with gave me the name of two companies in the United States that might cover me. After contacting both companies and finding the rates extremely high, I decided to take my chances of obtaining insurance in each country as I arrived.

I applied for my international drivers license and had it in a couple of days. I also had to obtain a "Carnet de Passage" for my motorcycle. Finding someone who knew what this document was all about, and how to obtain it, was the biggest problem. I made many phone calls and visited several Canadian Automobile Association offices in Edmonton before receiving the proper information. The *carnet de passage* is prepared by the CAA and guarantees the import tax to another country if I should sell my bike while in that country. That means putting up a guarantee of money to cover the import tax for the country with the highest import tax rate. Of course I had no plans of selling my bike along the way, but the document is still required and makes it easier to cross borders.

After providing the clerk at CAA, Ottawa, with all the details of my bike and a list of countries I would be traveling in, she informed me that I would need to put up a guarantee of thirty thousand dollars. The country with the highest import tax rate was Malaysia at 300 percent. I was not prepared to do that so I asked her what the next highest rate was. It was Singapore at 103 percent. That would make my guarantee $10,300.

Of course the clerk asked how I would get from Singapore to Thailand without riding through Malaysia. I told her I would worry about that when I got there. I have great admiration for the person I dealt with. Once she had all the information she required, the carnet was produced and sent out to me quickly, along with some valuable information about traveling abroad.

I renewed my passport early as to make it valid for five years. I did not plan to be gone that long, but my passport would expire in two years so I felt it was a good idea.

While I was taking care of all these issues, I was also learning how to build a Web site. Having no experience, I called on some of my friends in the biking community. I also called on a university friend of my son's, who is a computer whiz. With all their help I created a simple Web site that I would be able to update as I traveled.

www.untamedspirit.net

Now I had to make sure my little laptop was sufficient to handle all the pictures I planned to put on it. I bought a digital camera and would download all my photos onto the laptop. I had the computer upgraded with more hard drive and RAM. It should now take me through my whole trip, even if I were to get carried away taking pictures.

There were many days when I questioned everything I was doing. My fears would take hold and doubts would come flooding back in. Was it really wise for me to go traveling around the world on my motorcycle ... alone? Was it safe? Would I have enough money? Did I really want to spend all my hard earned savings? Would it be lonely without a travel companion? As these fears popped up something else would happen to brush them aside. I would meet people who have traveled extensively and be reassured by their stories, or someone would lend me a book on a country I really wanted to visit. Once again the excitement would build and my planning continued.

In June of 2001 I visited Gerbing's Heated Clothing in Union, Washington to have them sew a heated liner inside my riding jacket. When I told them of my plans to travel around the world, they supplied me with heated jacket and pant liners, heated gloves and socks and outer riding pants—all complimentary. My thanks go out to Gerbing's.

The last thing I had to do was to hold a garage sale and sell anything I was not storing with my children. I chose to dispose of almost everything except for a few personal belongings. I invited my daughter, sister and a couple of close friends to go through my clothes and take whatever they wanted. The clothes might as well be worn instead of stored in a box. Who knows, they might not be in style by the time I return.

My garage sale was held the weekend before I left and was very successful. I made a few dollars, which would help to start my journey. Once I sold my car I would be down to owning my motorcycle, the clothes and camping supplies for my travels and a few boxes of personal items. It was a scary feeling; but also liberating. I would soon be without a permanent place to live. My daughter and sisters were wonderful and said I could live with them when I got back. That was reassuring and made me feel good.

With the garage sale over I could concentrate on what to pack. First my clothes ... what do you take when you're going to be away for a couple of years? I had put a lot of thought into this, as I would be using only one small bag for clothes. Everything I took had to fit in one side saddlebag on the bike.

I laid everything out on the floor and then started to discard the things I could do without. In the end I had two pair of jeans (one to wear, one to pack), one pair of camping pants with zip off legs, three t-shirts (one long sleeved, two short), two tank tops, a bathing suit, a pair of pajamas, five pair of panties and socks and two bras (one I wore and one I packed). Not much, but that was all the room I had. My cosmetic bag went from being a large bag stuffed full to a very small bag not so stuffed. This all went into one side saddlebag.

The other side bag carried things for the bike—like a spare chain, two emergency tire inflating cans, spark plugs, oil filter, small package of camp pots including a dish and cup, my heated pant liners and socks, a first aide kit and a few other small items.

Next task was my camping gear. I had a tent, self-inflating mattress, sleeping bag, little camp pillow and bike cover. All this went into two rolls strapped behind my seat and in front of the trunk. In the trunk I put my laptop, all the chords and cables for the computer and digital camera, small umbrella, my blue jean jacket, extra gloves, leather neck-dickey, my carnet documents, a cable for locking the bike, runners, and a bottle of water.

My tank bag contained maps, camera, binoculars, purse (which fastened around my waist), travel guidebook, *GWRRA Gold Book* (a directory of all the Goldwing Road Rider Association members around the world), compass, camping knife, locks for the bike, et cetera. A small leather bag attached to the front forks held bike polish, windshield cleaner and chain lube. I knew exactly where everything went. Each item had its spot.

Whatever else came with me, I wore. My riding gear consisted of a jacket made from good waterproof fabric including a liner wired to provide heat, riding pants of the same waterproof material that zipped up the sides from ankle to hip (very convenient), riding boots which doubled as hiking boots, good leather riding gloves and a flip-up full face helmet. Oh yes, and a *silky* cap to wear under my helmet.

I set August 4 as the day I would leave. I would go to Canmore and spend a few days with my daughter Carey and grandson Bailey. Bailey is my youngest grandson, only one and a half years old. If I'm gone two years, he will have changed the most when I return.

The days before departure were hectic. I was not sure that I would get it all done. On the last night I was still sending things off with my son Brad and daughter-in-law, Carrie. I knew I could delay my departure if I wanted to, but I also knew that there would always be a reason to put it off. Instead, I told myself that whatever was not done, I would delegate to someone.

So that is what brings me to today, August 4, 2001—the start of my journey around the world …

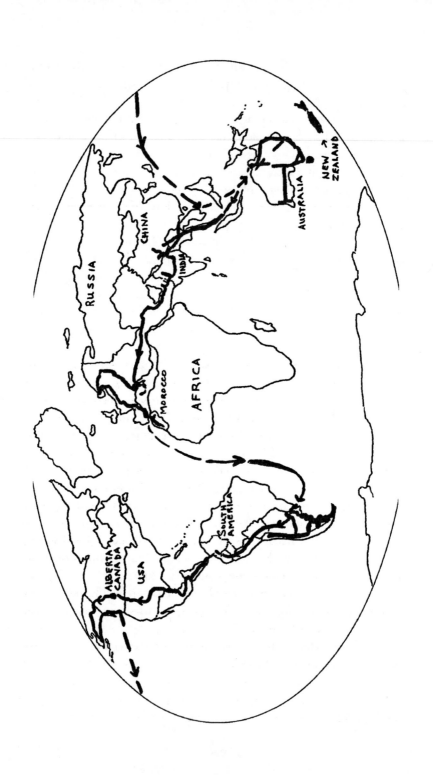

Chapter 1

Alberta to Alaska
Via the Great Alaska Highway

Here it is, August 4, 2001, the sun is shining and I am about to begin a whole new life. With my tent and sleeping bag strapped to the back of my bike, I ride off, leaving the comforts of the place I called home for almost six years. I have already experienced the doubts about selling everything I owned to travel around the world on my motorcycle, so this morning I only feel excitement. I am sure the doubts will come and go many more times as they have over the past several months.

What a glorious day to start my journey. The sun is shining over the city of Edmonton and there is no need to plug in my Gerbing's heated clothing. Once I pass Red Deer the clouds start to build on both sides of the highway. There seems to be a pathway of sunshine above me that remains right up to Canmore. It appears the universe is providing for me right from the moment I leave home.

I will be spending a few days in Canmore waiting for my "Carnet de Passage" to come from the Canadian Automobile Association in Ottawa. This is an important document required for crossing borders with a vehicle. While I wait I will spend some quality time with my daughter and grandson. I know I will miss them a lot, but just think of the stories I'll have to share with them when I return.

On Wednesday, August 8, the *carnet* finally arrives and I get my gear ready to strap onto the bike for an early morning departure.

Thursday morning brings some unexpected feelings. I am feeling particularly scared and vulnerable as I realize this is really it! Today I will really be heading out on my own into unknown territory. I am leaving my family behind and probably won't see them for two years. All the old fears come flooding in and I feel very much alone. I force myself to push the feelings aside, take in a deep breath, square my shoulders and get on with it.

My route takes me through the Columbia Icefields Parkway, which I have traveled many times. Once again I am in awe of the scenery. Highway 93 runs through the Rocky Mountains connecting Banff, Lake Louise and Jasper, boasting stunning views of mountains in excess of three thousand meters, the Athabasca glacier, and numerous colorful lakes. If you have never traveled this highway, you must do so—the landscape is truly magnificent! It is one of my favorite roads. I have traveled it by motorcycle in the summer and in spring, when part of the road was blocked by a snow slide. I have traveled it by car in the early fall when there has just been a recent snowfall and I have traveled it in winter. Driving through these mountains with the sun glistening off the fresh white snow is absolutely magical. Brown grizzlies and a black bears roam through here, and of course, the mountain goats and sheep are almost always somewhere along the route. I smile as I ride along remembering the wonderful trips through here with fellow bikers. My earlier fears begin to fade.

I stop early in Jasper and pull into Whistler's campground. The gate attendant warns me about keeping food and cosmetics locked up, as there has been a mother bear and two cubs roaming the area. I ask if wardens patrol the campground at night. The attendant assures me they do, so I set up camp and go into town for dinner and to shop for a couple of camping items. The evening is great for camping and I am ready for a good sleep. I am too tired to worry about the bears. I will just trust that the park patrol will keep us campers safe.

The morning gleams bright and sunny as I leave Jasper. Before I get out of the park I see an elk sporting a huge set of antlers and stop to take his picture. Just before reaching Hinton I turn onto Big Horn highway #40 leading to Grande Cache. I see a sign, *Kelly's Bathtub*, and decide to pull in and check it out. The trail takes me through tall trees and opens up on a beautiful little blue lake nestled between the mountains and trees, hidden from sight like a private bathtub. What a peaceful spot! This is definitely an ideal spot to spend a day hiking, picnicking, swimming and relaxing on the beach—but not today, another time.

I continue on to Grande Cache for a quick lunch stop, then on to Sulphur Gate just north of town. The name was recently changed from Hells Gate to Sulphur Gate. I take a gravel road off the highway for six kilometers, winding around the mountains and alongside the Smoky River, arriving at a parking area that appears to be a loading/ unloading point for horses. There is not a soul around. All I can see are a couple of empty horse trailers. The road continues farther down towards the river, but I park at the upper lot respecting the sign indicating no motorcycles. I am very nervous about bears but set out on a path through the bush anyway, determined to see this canyon. I pick out a trail that leads in the direction of the river and find myself hiking down a rather steep hill. As I hike I scan the bushes around me and keep a keen eye open for wildlife. I find myself talking just to make noise, after realizing I left my bear bells on the bike. Soon I reach the river, take a good look around for safety, and proceed to take pictures. The rock walls on either side of the river reach up some sixty to seventy meters creating a narrow passage known as Sulphur Gate or Little Hells Gate. What an incredible view—well worth the walk.

I had not realized how steep this hill was until I started my hike back up. Less than half way up I find myself panting like a person extremely out of shape. If I should encounter a bear right now, I would probably collapse from exhaustion. Now I am really getting nervous so I start to sing—that should keep the bears away! This is a huge forest with a lot of wildlife; and this year, 2001, the bear population in the mountains is at it's highest ever. I reach the parking lot safely and as I am about to leave I get the urge to ride down the road past the sign saying *motorcycles prohibited.* It just doesn't seem fair, so down I go. I encounter another parking lot with more horse trailers and a couple of cars. From here I can almost see the canyon through the trees. Once again I park my bike and decide to hike the trail. The last trail took me to the bottom of the canyon by the river; this one takes me to the top. Now I am hiking along the edge of the cliff overlooking the canyon and the river. I stop to take pictures along the way and am almost at the top when I hear a noise in the bushes to my left. My heart leaps! Seconds later two hikers come around the corner on their way back to the parking lot. *Whew! Relax Doris.* A couple more pictures and I retrace my steps to the bike. It is exactly where I left it—it has not been hauled away. Now that my nerves have settled down, I am glad I decided to do this little excursion. Sulphur Gate Canyon is a spectacular sight from the top and the bottom. A definite Kodak moment!

Back on the bike and on to Grande Prairie. I am having a little trouble staying awake so I take advantage of a couple of rest stops and close my eyes for a few minutes. The weather is gorgeous, the road smooth and the scenery incredible! About 5:00 PM I reach Grande Prairie, fuel up my bike and pull out my GWRRA *Gold Book*. This book is a directory of motorcycle riders around the world who belong to the Gold Wing Road Rider Associations. The first person on the list is David Chomik. I call and get his wife Elizabeth on the phone and ask if they might want to go riding for the weekend. She informs me that their daughter is getting married tomorrow and they have family coming in tonight. At this point she puts David on the phone and he insists I come out to meet them. I protest, not wanting to interrupt their family gathering, but he won't hear a word of it. So I relinquish my argument and take his directions. I ride about ten kilometers out of town and arrive at their acreage. David and Elizabeth invite me to stay for the evening and offer me a bed. Again I protest, but they insist, so here I am at a very casual pre-wedding party with some of the nicest people I have ever met. The Chomiks would be the first of many wonderful people around the world who open their homes to me.

Next morning I leave Grande Prairie for Dawson Creek, British Columbia. My first stop is to get a picture of the "Mile 0" signpost—signifying the start of the Great Alaska Highway.

This highway was constructed in 1942, in a period of eight months, and runs for 2,450 kilometers (1,523 miles) from Dawson Creek to Fairbanks Alaska. I ride through this scenic country to Fort Nelson, B.C. before stopping for the night. Just as I am climbing the last hill into town, I run out of fuel. Thank goodness for the spare gas can that is strapped to my bike. The only complaint I have about my new bike is the small fuel tank.

The sun is still with me as I leave Fort Nelson. I feel great after a good night sleep and ready for an adventurous day. As I am cruising through the mountains I can't help but think how vibrant this scene will be in a month's time when the leaves start to turn color. My first stop for fuel is at Tetsa River, BC. I really luck out stopping here. The cook has just taken a batch of freshly baked cinnamon buns out of the oven. What a treat!

About five kilometers down the road I come across two cute little bambies that still have their spots. I slow right down so they have time to get off the road before the vehicles behind me approach. Another few kilometers down the road I round a curve and there, right in my path, is a black bear! In a fraction of a second my thoughts race—Do I slow down? Stop? *NO!* He would be on me before I could turn around. I quickly look around and don't see another bear; there is no traffic coming so I instantly I decide to keep my speed and go around him on the left. As I approach he raises up on his hind legs, his right shoulder and paw stretched high in the air. Is he coming my way ... or ... just then he turns and goes into the ditch on the right. *Wow!* That got the old heart pumping.

At Mile 496 I cross the Liard River Bridge, the only remaining suspension bridge on the Alaska Highway. I reach Liard River Hot Springs at about 3:00 PM and get a campsite. The bear population in these areas is the highest it's been in many years, so if I sound paranoid, it is for good reason. I ask the usual questions of the park ranger and am told there has been one hanging around the upper springs, but it has not come into the campground (that's not to say it won't). The lady I am questioning gives me a new tip on camping safety—"Walk around your tent to mark your territory," she says. "The wildlife will respect your space."

I pitch my tent and proceed to walk circles around my tent. I must admit my territory gets bigger with each circle. As I walk around and around I notice the grass and small bush at one edge of my campsite is packed down. Looks to me like an animal could have slept there last night. *Oh no, this can't be!* I take a good look around wondering if I should move my tent and all its contents. After a few moments of deep thought, I decide to stay right where I am. A few more circles around my tent and no animal will dare to invade my territory. That job done, it is time to relax and spend some time in the hot pools.

The evening is serene and it is a pleasant walk to the hot springs. I follow a boardwalk that crosses about thirty-five meters of swamp and continues through the trees. I stop briefly at the lower pools then carry on to the upper springs. Since I am camped in the campground a short distance away, I need to see for myself that there are no bears around. I remain very alert as I continue up the path leading to the upper pool. The pool is vacant except for two lovers taking advantage of the seclusion and the fact that most people will not chance coming up here. I do not plan on going into the upper pool so I leave them to their privacy and retrace my steps to the lower pool, change into my swimsuit, and join the handful of people soaking in the hot mineral water. These are natural springs flowing from the mountains and left in their natural setting. I sit on rocks kept clean by the flowing water. Ooh ... the water is so warm. This is just what I need to finish off a great day.

August 13, I have survived the night without a bear attack. I guess walking in circles for half an hour last night did the trick. I pack up and make my first stop for breakfast at mile 596 of the Alaska Highway; a little place called Iron Creek Lodge—another fortunate choice. I order pancakes and coffee and take a table on the patio overlooking a calm blue lake. The waitress tells me the lake has no name. In the fishing guidebooks it is referred to as Iron Creek Pothole. This little *pothole* is twenty-two meters (70 feet) deep in the middle and produces sixty-centimeter (24-inch) rainbow trout. I relax and enjoy the view and serenity.

At about noon I reach Watson Lake, Yukon, which is famous for the signs posted by travelers from around the world. A U.S. Army GI from Illinois started the forest in 1942 while working on the Alaska Highway. He erected a sign here pointing the way and stating the mileage to his hometown. Others followed his lead and are still doing so to this day. July 20, 1990, marked the ten thousandth sign in the forest. I make my sign to add to the display. I did not come prepared with one, so I inquire with the clerk at the information desk and she kindly offers me a slab of wood from the back of her truck. I break it with my boot to the length I need then proceed to make my sign. There are several Edmonton signs here already so I decide to write BROWNFIELD ALBERTA, Doris Maron, 2001. Brownfield is the little farming community where I grew up. My guess is there won't be a sign spouting *Brownfield* amongst this sign forest ... now there is. This is an interesting place and I spend an hour just reading names on signs placed here by visitors from around the world. The construction of signs is of a great variety. Everything from stolen road signs, license plates, custom-made marble, wood, stone, tin foil plates, and rough hand made signs like mine.

I continue on to Mukluk Annie's for the night. Camping is free and they offer a salmon bake every night. I have a small order with salad bar, baked beans and fresh bread all for $16.00. The price also includes a boat cruise across the lake. My camping spot is on the bank overlooking Teslin Lake. The view, when I look out my tent, is of the lake framed by mountains with the sun setting in the background. What more could I ask for!

The following morning over breakfast I spend some time visiting with a retired couple from California. He has a 1995 Goldwing, but right now they are traveling in their motor home. I love to hear stories from people who are enjoying their retirement.

Today my destination is Whitehorse. I pass by Marsh Lake—the most beautiful deep, rich blue lake I have ever seen. About thirty kilometers out of Whitehorse I cross the Yukon River. On my way into town I see a sign to Mile Canyon and decide to take this winding road. It passes the city's water reservoir and continues up to a lookout point that overlooks a narrow canyon and the river below. Today a film crew is working on the banks of the river and I am told they are shooting a Ford commercial.

When I ride into Whitehorse I search out the Honda dealer to get my bike serviced. I try a couple of numbers from the *Gold Book* and reach Elma Rehn. She works just a few blocks away and invites me to her office. She offers me a spot to pitch my tent in her yard, which is out of town sixty kilometers. Later that evening I meet Al Higgens, also a member of GWRRA, and the three of us enjoy sharing bike stories for the evening. What a wonderful world, full of friends I have not yet met.

I spend a couple of days in Whitehorse before leaving for Dawson City with my newfound friends Elma and Al. It's great having travel companions for the day. Our first stop is Braeburn Lodge for coffee and a cinnamon bun. One bun is big enough to feed all three of us—and oh, so delicious! When we reach Dawson City we set up camp before going sight seeing. Al shows us around town and some local spots of interest. We visit the dredge, the cemetery, and the Hill (also called the Dome). What a fabulous view from the Dome. With my binoculars I can spot our campsite far below and to the left. To the right I locate

Dawson City and the Yukon River. Across the river is the road I will take tomorrow leading to the *Top of the World Highway*. What an awesome view! We top off the evening at Diamond Tooth Gerdie's Saloon to watch the showgirls dance and listen to the vocals of D. T. Gerdie. Dawson City is like riding back in time to the old, wild, west.

Saturday, August 18, is two weeks since I left home. I experience an exhilarating feeling of freedom, knowing I don't have to be home in a week or two.

I leave Dawson City after a leisurely breakfast with my new friends from Whitehorse. We say our goodbyes and I ride down the riverbank to the ferry, just in time to board before the chain is pulled across. The ferry is nothing more than a raft and I am boarded with six vehicles and one bicycle. In less than fifteen minutes we dock on the other bank and I ride off to the Top of the World Highway. I experience a rush of excitement mixed with apprehension as I head across the mountains on my own. The road switches back and forth as I climb higher and higher. I left Dawson City in sunshine, but now the clouds are starting to accumulate. The road is good; paved in most places and hard packed gravel in others. After a few miles of climbing I look out across the tops of the trees and realize I am at eye level with the mountain peaks on the other side of the valley. What a breathtaking view! Forested mountains and coulees stretch ahead of me—I can see for miles. Small sections of the highway are visible as it winds through the trees and around the mountains. The only cut lines I see in the forest are those of the road cutting through trees at the tops of the mountains. I can easily imagine how colorful this will be in a couple of weeks when the leaves start to turn. Soon I reach the summit at an elevation of 1,376 meters (4,515 ft) on the Canadian side, then round the top of a mountain and begin a short decline to the Canadian/USA border—Poker Creek crossing. Poker Creek is one hundred and five kilometers (sixty-six miles) from Dawson City and sits at 1,258 meters (4,127 ft) above sea level.

The border crossing is small and I am cleared without delay. I travel about thirty kilometers before the road shows signs of a recent rain. I have long since left the pavement but still find the road not bad to ride on. I continue optimistically. This does not last long and soon I am into *very* wet roads. I feel my rear wheel slip, reminding me to keep it steady. I pray that I don't drop my bike. The road is atrocious for the next fifty kilometers. My bike fishtails when I have to cross a muddy track to make room for an oncoming truck and camper. I am happy to safely reach the little town of Chicken and get off the road for a short break. I stop for fuel and a lunch of chicken soup—an appropriate choice for being in a town called Chicken, Alaska. It has stopped raining for a bit and I am told there is only twenty-two miles to go before the new chip seal surface. I head out again and battle the remaining stretch of mud. The clouds look like they are breaking up and I am ever so thankful when I reach the hard surface. The remainder of my trip to Tok is much more relaxing. My bike and I are filthy, so after I fuel up, I give the bike a quick spray off and unload a pack of mud before continuing on to Delta Junction for the night.

My first stop on August 19 is at North Pole, Alaska. I stop at Elves Den restaurant for brunch before touring the Santa Claus House. Every toy imaginable is in here. My thoughts go to my grandchildren as I imagine their excitement if they were here. I take a ride through town and am thrilled to see candy cane light poles and Christmas decorations lining the streets. Remember, this is August. From here I continue on to Fairbanks where I visit the Moving Memorial Wall and pay tribute to the thousands of fallen soldiers—truly a moving event. I seek out the visitor center and find there is a lot to do in Fairbanks. This might be a good place to stay a day or two. As I am talking to the clerk she notices my heater cord hanging from my jacket and asks, "My goodness, what are you plugged into dearie?"

I chuckle and explain that I plug it into my bike for heat while I am riding. She is totally amazed. Loaded with sightseeing information I take a walk through Alaskaland, a unique park depicting the early days of Fairbanks.

At about 4:00 PM I look for a room, as there is still a lot I would like to see here. There is a bicycle charity ride for Aids starting from Fairbanks tomorrow and it seems the whole town is booked solid. Approximately two thousand cyclists are participating in the ride. The temperature is a little too cool to pitch my tent tonight so I decide to ride on to Healy for the night. That will put me closer to Denali Park for the morning.

Up early to arrive at Denali by 7:00 AM. All the early bus tours are booked except a twelve-hour tour leaving at 8:30. I buy my ticket and return to the bike to lock it up. It looks like a clear day and a possibility of seeing the top of Mt. McKinley.

Just before 8:30 AM I board the bus along with about thirty other tourists. Our bus driver, Virgie, introduces herself and states that she is not a tour guide but will share all her knowledge of the area. She has lived in these parts all her life and does a great job of giving us historical information about the park and Alaska. We are only in the park a short distance before we spot two caribou. Caribou are plentiful out here and we see several throughout the day. The road soon turns to gravel and Virgie informs us it will become one-lane gravel as we get farther into the park and climb higher up the mountains. We spot some dall sheep on the side of a mountain and soon one of the passengers spots a bear off to the left. Virgie pulls the bus over and gives us a chance to pull out the binoculars. Sure enough, there is a big, blond grizzly and her cub. Magnificent animals!

We start to climb the steep road up the mountainside. The road is getting narrower and Virgie points out the road ahead winding higher and clinging to the edge of the mountain. I would not want to be riding my bike up here. The buses all run with their 4-way flashers on, stop prior to rounding the curve of the mountain, and honk to be sure another vehicle is not coming. We spot a couple of moose and another grizzly, this time with two cubs. We are stopped very high up the side of the mountain. All of a sudden we notice two trekkers down below walking parallel to the road. They are not far from the grizzly and we wonder if they see the bear. She looks up, spots them and takes a couple of steps in their direction; but she has two cubs in the bushes so does not pursue the hikers. The trekkers keep on walking at a steady pace, not looking to either side. I am sure they know the bear is there but their only option is to keep walking and hope she ignores them. Traveling farther into the park we spot a couple of moose and fox. The only animal we do not see is the illusive wolf.

One of the main attractions going through Denali Park is seeing the peak of Mt. McKinley, the highest mountain in North America.

At 20,320 feet high, ninety percent of the time the peak is behind clouds. Well guess what! Today is clear enough that we are able to see and photograph Mt. McKinley. The scenery throughout the park is a photographers dream. I notice many people carrying expensive photography equipment and setting up tripods on the edge of high mountain cliffs.

On the way back down the mountain I am sitting on the cliff side of the bus. I realize now how narrow the road is. Looking down, we estimate a thousand meters or more straight down into the valley. The clouds are rolling in and there is a storm coming. Virgie wastes no time getting the bus on the road. We have another two hours back to base and the visitor center. I would hate to be caught on these roads in a thundering rainstorm. We make it back safely and the clouds have lightened slightly. The time is 8:30 PM and I still have to find a place to stay. I ride a short distance to Grizzly Bear Campground and find a spot for my tent amongst many other campers. Now isn't that a brave move!

I have been enjoying my days of riding with very little traffic on the highways, when suddenly I realize there are a lot of vehicles again. I look around and wonder where they all came from, then realize I am nearing Anchorage. I arrive in the city at about 4:00 PM and once again refer to my *Gold Book*. Pat and Bob Anderson are first on the list, and Pat invites me to stay in their home. They are great people and help me make some contacts for my flight to Japan then on to Australia. After two days of phone calls I determine that the cost to fly and ship my bike from Anchorage to Japan, then on to Australia, is more than four times as much as the cost from Vancouver to Australia. After some deliberation I decide to omit Japan for now. I will travel to Haines, Alaska, take the ferry to Prince Rupert and ride to Vancouver. From Vancouver I will make arrangements to ship my bike to Australia. I make a booking on the ferry at Haines for August 26 and then do some last minute sightseeing in Anchorage before nightfall.

August 24 I awake to a cloudy and rainy day. Late morning I say my goodbyes to Pat & Bob and take the Old Glenn Highway (#1) to Glenallen then Tok. If you were to ask any of the locals how to get to the number 1 highway, chances are they would not know. They refer to highways by name rather than number.

The weather today is a mixture of sun and clouds with rainy periods.

At one point, past Glenallen, I marvel at the sun hitting the mountains on my left and the rain coming down between the mountains on my right. It has warmed up a bit and I am quite comfortable. I would like to cross the Canadian border tonight so as to shorten my day tomorrow.

At Tok, Alaska, I stop just long enough for fuel, juice and a bathroom break. Rain is coming down lightly but I decide to continue and head southeast on the Alcan Highway. It is getting late and the rain is hitting harder now. Clouds overhead are very dark and I begin to question my decision to press on. For the second time since I left home I feel very alone and vulnerable. I seem to be the only person on the road for miles and miles. *Why didn't I follow my plan not to ride after dark?*

Shortly I meet a couple of vehicles and wonder what the occupants might be thinking, seeing a biker on the highway this dark evening in the pouring rain. Do they think I'm crazy and freezing to death? Maybe they feel sorry for me. I smile at that thought, feeling quite cozy with my electric gear turned on and my silky covering my head under my helmet. I notice the sky across the mountains to my left is not so dark. In fact, there are actually some blue patches showing through. I hope the road winds in that direction.

Luck is with me. As I ride a few more curves around the mountains the blue patches get closer. Before long I am into lighter skies. I glance up at the mountains and see the most awesome northern lights. A mixture of colors ranging from yellow, green, purple and red splash like paint across the sky. Each vibrant color blends into the next, brushing the mountaintop. These must be the northern lights Alaska brags about.

I reach the border crossing at Beaver Creek, Yukon, at about 9:00 PM, fuel my bike, and then grab a bowl of soup and a dorm-type room for thirty-five dollars. It has been a long day and I am ready to crash.

Next morning I sleep in and do not leave Beaver Creek until 10:00. Yesterday was more tiring than I thought. Today the sky is clearing and the sun is taking over. My first stop is Destruction Bay for lunch. I find a restaurant with windows facing Kluane Lake so I can enjoy the view. The lake is a beautiful deep cobalt blue; the water is calm and not a boat in sight. I cannot help but ask why, and the waiter tells me they offer boat tours on the lake all summer, but business is slow right now as tourist season is winding down for the year.

Continuing on from Destruction Bay the road climbs higher and the lake appears turquoise from above. I spot another bear—this time running across the road in front of oncoming traffic. As I approach, he is running across the ditch about ten meters to my right, disappearing into the bushes.

I follow along Kluane Lake for about forty-five kilometers. What a gorgeous ride, both scenery and road. Toward the end of the lake I encounter a road construction crew. I ride safely through two bad stretches before I can relax and enjoy the colorful countryside. For a long stretch I'm thinking this must be gravel country because the ditches seem to be full of smooth round rocks. After a closer look I realize these rocks are actually dandelion gone to seed, and the tops are now puffballs. Farther along the fireweed take over the ditches and gleam a bright red against the green, yellow and orange leaves. The leaves are just starting to turn color. Wherever the fireweed is turning to seed the ditches look pink. What a delightful scene!

As I ride around the last few curves going into Haines, my bike sputters and dies—out of fuel again! I push it close to the edge, as there is no place to pull off this narrow, winding road. I look around to make sure there are no signs of bear, then very quickly pour the spare fuel into the tank. I know the bear are plentiful out here and I would not want to encounter one while my bike is immobile.

Back on the road I travel about two kilometers before reaching Haines. Now, wouldn't you think the fuel could have held out for two kilometers? Anyway … Haines is a quaint little town built around a bay at the waters edge and nestled in the mountains. I find a room, stroll around town a bit to see the sights, have a bite to eat and go to bed.

Next morning I'm up early to arrive at the ferry by 7:00. I look forward to this two-day ride on the Alaska marine highway from Haines to Prince Rupert. Once my bike is secured I search out the Solarium deck and drop my sleeping bag to lay claim to a hard, plastic lounge chair. This will be my bed for the night. I am not alone; there are about twenty loungers lined up against the wall, all filled with gear of other passengers who do not wish to pay for a stateroom. The loungers are in an outer passageway that is open to the viewing deck. The roof extends over far enough to keep the rain from pouring down on us. The day starts out clear enough to see the surrounding mountains, but by evening the clouds have socked in and rain comes steadily down. It rains most of the night and I am thankful to be on board this ship and not riding. As the rain comes down it floods the floor where we sleep so we must make sure our things are picked up and put in the lockers behind us. Sometime during the night the feel of the ship rocking breaks my sleep. The rain continues to fall and I am surprised at how warm it feels out here.

Morning comes and it has quit raining, but the sky is still cloudy. We are docked at Ketchikan for a short stop. Occasionally I take out my binoculars and watch for whales—with no success. It will be late afternoon before we dock in Prince Rupert, British Columbia.

Chapter 2

British Columbia, Canada

The ferry docks in Prince Rupert at 4:30 PM on August 27. Upon leaving the ferry I ride east through the mountains on Highway 16 to a visitors centre. I am looking for cheap accommodation tonight to compensate for the cost of the ferry. The attendant directs me to North Pacific Historic Fishing Village where I will find a hostel. The village is five kilometers past Port Edward, a short distance south of Highway 16. It looks deserted, but I was told to go to the restaurant and someone would meet me. I wander down the boardwalks, between two rows of old buildings and finally find the restaurant. Yes, they are expecting me, and someone will be over shortly to show me to my room.

While I wait I order a salad and chat with the cook. He is a friendly chap. I tell him about my tire dilemma—I have noticed the back one is wearing fast. He proceeds to make a couple of phone calls to find someone who can help me. It turns out the closest place is Terrace, 135 kilometers away. Let me tell you how good people are; the cook's friend offers to drive to Terrace to pick up the tires if I feel it is too dangerous to ride further. I assure them I don't think that is necessary, but I am extremely grateful for the offer.

Shortly Keri, the manager, arrives and takes me to see my room. The "Miki Bunkhouse" is their hostel accommodations. Keri leads me down the boardwalk to the end of a long row of old buildings (shacks). Those on our right are built on stilts extending out over the water. Those on our left are built into the bank and even have a small lawn with a short picket fence. Everything is in desperate need of painting. As we approach the last building I begin to worry. This building has a window broken out on one side and is in the biggest need of repair.

That can't be the building, I'm thinking. We reach the end of the walk ... *it is the Miki Bunkhouse!* I cannot help but feel a little nervous.

We enter the bunkhouse and Keri shows me around. On the main floor there's a kitchen, little sitting room, bathroom and three bedrooms, each containing triple bunk beds. The second floor has four bedrooms each containing triple bunks. The broken window is in a part of the house that is boarded off. Since I am the only guest I can take my pick of rooms. The only other person staying here tonight is one of the employees. I cannot help but ask why there is no one around. Keri tells me the staff members are across the lake at an employee barbeque, to celebrate the end of the season.

My mind is racing. Do I or don't I? The thought occurs to me that I am going to see far worse than this before I complete my journey around the world. With that I decide to stay. Keri gives me the combination to the padlock on the main door and tells me to lock it if I should go out walking. *Oh dear, what am I getting myself into?* I remind myself how friendly and helpful the cook was earlier. *I'll be okay.*

I choose the bedroom off the kitchen, next to the bathroom, lock the house and go back to the bike to get my things. The distance back to the parking lot is a good hike, so I take only what I need for the night and head back to my bunkhouse. Once I have my things deposited in my room and my sleeping bag arranged, I decide to go exploring. When I pull my bedroom door closed I discover it does not latch. On closer inspection, it doesn't even have the inner parts to make it latch. An inspection of the other rooms tells me they are no better. Not even the bathroom door latches. In fact, there is no doorknob, just a hole where the doorknob should be! I'll worry about all this later; right now I want to take a walk before it gets too dark.

I stroll up the boardwalk past the restaurant and towards the museum. I notice there has been some building improvements made to both the restaurant and the museum and another larger building across the boardwalk from the restaurant. This one is called the Hotel. Rooms here start at eighty dollars a night. You can also rent individual cabins for about fifty-five dollars. From the outside they look very much like the house I am staying in. The price for a room in the Miki Bunkhouse is ten dollars.

Back in my room, the place is still empty so I have a quick shower. I prop my tank bag up against the door to compensate for the missing doorknob—as if that would stop anyone from getting in! Shower complete, I relax and write in my journal.

About 9:30 PM my housemate arrives. I meet James, a young man from the prairies who is the second cook for the village. James came here for the summer months to work and experience a different part of Canada before going back home to college. I admire these young people with their adventurous spirit and courage to spread their wings. At that age I was just too afraid to stray too far from home. James is the first of many courageous young people I will meet along my travels.

I am not completely comfortable without a lock on my bedroom door, so when I retire for the night I prop my chair under the doorknob and drop all my belongings against the door. Not the Hilton, but I have a bed, four walls around me and a roof over my head with a three-inch hole in one corner of the ceiling. The view out my bedroom window is delightful. I look out on the Skeena River surrounded by mountains and pines, and can hear water running from the mountainside into the river below me. What more could I ask for? Another place or time it could be a romantic getaway. Port Edward is located on the Tsimpsean Peninsula, 565 kilometers (350 miles) northwest of Vancouver and approximately eighty kilometers (fifty miles) from the Alaska border.

August 28 I awake to sunshine. I pay for my room and inquire about their museum. Two big busloads of tourists have arrived for breakfast and a tour of the museum. The place is busy. I am sure the exhibits are interesting, but I'm anxious to get to a bike shop for tires so I do not stay.

I stop at bike shops in every town along my route just to find that no one has tires to fit my bike. Shops are already gearing up for the winter season and replacing their motorcycles with snowmobiles. My rear tire tread is disappearing fast; but the sun is shining and I don't have to worry about wet roads. About fifty kilometers north of Smithers I come across another black bear on the side of the road. As I make my way past he is the width of a lane away from me. A couple of vehicles are stopped, the occupants watching him. I reach Burns Lake—still no tires. The owner of the shop here inspects my tires and assures me I will be okay until Prince George. Evening is approaching quickly so I find a KOA and camp for the night.

I reach Prince George the next day around noon and call the Honda dealer. Not much help there. The gal I speak to tells me to call the Yamaha dealer. Okay, so no one has tires for my bike. My only option is to have the Yamaha dealer order a set for me. To my surprise and good fortune, the tires arrive next morning and the Yamaha shop has me back on the road in short order. Great service!

I spend a couple of days in Prince George making contact with other bikers and visiting cousins I have never met before. What a great treat that is, meeting family members for the first time. Second cousins, George and Eddie, invite me to stay with them. They show me around town and urge me to come back some winter to experience dog sledding. That sounds like great fun.

I contact Ron and Carol Meyers from the Prince George GWRRA and they invite me on the *Gold Run* to Clinton for the weekend. I am looking forward to riding with them. Bright and early Saturday morning, September 1, I meet the group of Goldwing riders and welcome the change to ride with a group again. This ride is an annual event and weekend campout. The registration includes a draw for prizes, a corn roast, and deep fried turkey. Mmm, is that good! That afternoon I check my entry ticket and find I have won a set of Italian air horns. One of the Prince George members installs them on my bike, so look out fellow motorists—they are loud! Sunday morning is pancake breakfast and awards. What a great day for a short ride. Some riders go on the poker run, while others tour the beautiful countryside.

Monday, the end of the long weekend, I ride to Abbotsford where I will stay with Kathryn for a few days. Kathryn is a good friend and riding companion who traveled across the USA and Canada with me in year 2000. I think of how great it would be if she could join me on my world trip—but that is not to be.

The ride down the Fraser Canyon is wonderful, even though the wind gusts push at me occasionally. I am glad to be riding on new tires. My thoughts drift to Australia and the arrangements that have to be made to ship my bike.

September 7 Kathryn and I pack up our bikes for a three-day ride. For me this is one last ride before shipping my bike to Australia. Monday it goes into the packaging depot to be crated and shipped. But today the sun is shining and it promises to be a great weekend.

Our route takes us north on Highway 1 through Hope and on to Hells Gate. We take the tram down to the bottom of the canyon, which provides an awesome view from this point. We walk across the swinging bridge, meander through the shops, and then watch a video on the migration of the salmon. Huge cement gateways have been built on each side of the Fraser River to protect the fish as they migrate upstream. Water, at this narrow passage, rushes through at 800 million liters per second. Before the gateways were built, most of the fish never survived the brutal force of the water. Now about 90 percent make it through. The canyon is 33.5 meters (110 feet) wide and today the water is 39.6 meters (130 feet) deep.

Back on our bikes we continue on to Cache Creek. The sun has cast a shadow across our side of the canyon, but on the other side the mountains still glimmer in sunlight. We locate a campground in Cache Creek and set up camp. The evening is cool so we make a fire and relax with a bottle of wine.

Up early to a cool morning, but the sun is already promising to warm the day. We have breakfast then head out towards Lillooet via Highway 99. This will take us through the marble canyon on an excellent biking road. I wish I had a camera mounted to my helmet to capture the shots I can't stop to get. It seems like the most picturesque landscape shots happen when we are unable to stop.

We have lunch in Lillooet then continue on Highway 99 to

Pemberton. Passing Duffy Lake without stopping to take photos is impossible. This is amongst some of the most gorgeous countryside in western Canada. We arrive in Pemberton and attend a campout and pig roast with another group of bikers. What a great bunch of people! Sometime during the evening someone mentions that they saw a bear during their walk today. Needless to say this makes some of us who are tenting a little nervous. Kathryn and I quickly claim the garage as our campsite and move both our tents inside. We take a lot of ribbing that evening and next morning, but we are safe and warm.

Sunday morning, after breakfast with the group, we continue south on highway 99 to Vancouver. We make a stop at Whistler for an hour, just to browse around. It has sure changed since I was there last—some twenty-five years ago. Next stop is Porteau Cove for a snack and pictures. We end up in a traffic jam going across North Vancouver but eventually make it back to Abbotsford, satisfied with our fabulous weekend ride.

Monday morning, September 10, I ride my bike, with Kathryn following in her car, to the Packaging Depot to prepare for shipment to Melbourne, Australia. I am told it will go out on Friday the 14. I disconnect the battery, tape the terminals and connectors, remove the windshield and mirrors, and drain the fuel from the bike as well as my portable gas can.

Once all the paperwork is complete, and I have hassled the gentleman with my many concerns, we leave. As we are walking to the car I can't help but look back several times. I cannot begin to explain the feeling of leaving my bike there. I feel like I am leaving my first-born child for the very first time! It feels like there are too many loose ends, like I am putting too much trust in these people. I guess I thought I would watch them crate it up right there in front of me and see it loaded on the ship. How silly of me.

September 11, 2001, a few minutes before 8:00 AM I turn on the TV (which is something I have not done for a month) and see **"AMERICA UNDER ATTACK"** across the screen. The World Trade Center is exploding! My first thought is, *what kind of a movie are they advertising now?* For two days I sit glued to the TV, as I am sure most of the world does, and watch replays of this tragic event. It is difficult to digest the magnitude of what is happening. All of a sudden I feel a long way from home and I haven't even left Canada yet.

Once again I find myself questioning whether or not to continue my journey. *Should I phone the Packaging Depot and cancel my shipment?* I know the bike hasn't left the depot yet. In the next few days my thoughts run wild. If I cancel now, I may never fulfill this dream. If I let this stop me, what will be the next obstacle that stops me? After about five days of soul searching I decide to continue with my plans. Life must go on and we each do what we must.

September 14, I phone to see if my bike is loaded and ready to be shipped out. "No" is the answer I get. "It won't leave the port until the 23rd." This is not surprising news—I was expecting the delay with the World Trade Center tragedy. This means arrival in Melbourne November 9. Quite obviously I am being given a lesson in patience.

I make my flight arrangements to Australia—I will fly out of Vancouver October 27, arriving in Melbourne on the 29. That will give me more time to visit with my son, Curtis, and his girlfriend, Vanessa, in Melbourne before picking up my bike and beginning my tour of Australia. As for now, I have time to fly home and spend a couple of weeks with my family.

Chapter 3

Australia, Part I

Finally October 27 arrives and I am on my way to Australia. Cathay Pacific Airlines is the way to fly—very spacious and excellent service. I am impressed.

The first leg of my flight is thirteen hours and eight minutes, covering 10,282 kilometers (6,272 miles) of the globe. I leave Vancouver at 2:20 PM, October 27 and will arrive in Hong Kong at 6:35 PM October 28. I will have lost half a day.

Excitement is running high and sleep eludes me so I watch the world pass by below. As we fly over Alaska I spot Mt. McKinley, the highest mountain in North America. As we fly farther north over Siberia I am able to see the smoke or steam coming from the volcanoes. I watch the small monitor in front of me and note that we have climbed to 9,400 meters, the temperature is minus 54 degrees Celsius and the time is 6:30 PM Pacific time. A couple of hours later our altitude is 10,800 meters.

The temperature upon landing at Hong Kong airport is 27 degrees. I have a five-hour layover here before boarding again for Melbourne. The Hong Kong airport is impressive, much bigger than any I have ever been in. I wander through some of the many shops before finding a coffee shop. I'm shocked at the price of a cup of coffee. At 11:45 PM I am flying again, another eight hours and forty minutes, to my final destination.

October 29, 2001, the time is 11:35 AM. When we touch down

the pilot announces 15 degrees Celsius in Melbourne. An hour to claim my bags, clear quarantine and customs, and I am on the other side embracing my son, Curtis, and his girlfriend, Vanessa. This is an absolute thrill after more than two years separation. Curtis left Canada in July of 1999 to go to Australia for a year. He liked it enough to apply for permanent residency.

What is my first impression of Australia? It feels great to be out without a winter coat and boots. Everything is green with flowers in full bloom. I especially notice all the roses. The buildings are of Victorian style architecture, many built in the 1800's and early 1900's. It's wonderful to see the preservation of these beautiful structures. The passenger side of the car is on the left and people drive like maniacs. Pedestrians look out for their own safety and do not assume the right of way. Maybe that is how it should be. I have to listen very intently to conversations in order to understand people. Australians have a British style accent that my ear is not accustomed to. I am soon to discover that Melbourne is a very expensive city to live in with a lot of wealth passed down through the generations.

Next morning I leave early with Curtis and Vanessa and get my first introduction to using the train to go into the city. *The City* is the term Australians use when referring to *downtown*. I check in with immigration to see about extending my visa from three months to a year and get some very good news. Since I am going to New Zealand January 20th I can get my visa renewed for three months electronically, at no additional cost, before I return. I am also told that if I want to extend it for an additional period the fee is less if I apply before coming back to Australia ($60 versus $180). I can apply for an extension while in New Zealand.

I find my way back to Peter Stevens Motorcycle Shop, where Curtis works, and receive more good news. Australian Groupage Service has sent over a fax stating that my bike will arrive in Sydney Friday, November 2. That means I will be able to pick it up by November 9 from Secon, a shipping warehouse, in Melbourne.

With this great news I go out and explore the city. There is a lot to see and do in the city of Melbourne. I wander through Meyer mall with the dome skylight and famous clock. The clock opens up every hour to expose black birds singing Waltzing Matilda. The city core has a lot of great shops, all of which are quite crowded with people. I walk through the parliament grounds, past a stately old cathedral, through Flinders (bus) Station, across the Yarra River to Queen Victoria Park, and follow a footpath through the park. Beautifully kept parks are plentiful with walking and cycling trails that could keep you exploring for days.

November 6, Curtis and Vanessa take me out to the family beach house at Queenscliff, located south of Melbourne across Port Phillip Bay.

Today is Melbourne Cup day and a declared holiday. The Melbourne Cup is held on the first Tuesday in November every year. We unpack quickly upon arriving and go into town to place our bets on the race. I make my picks and bet a whole $12.00.

We pick up a few groceries then return to the beach house in time to watch a couple of races before the big one. It is amazing how exciting a race can be when you have placed a bet—even a $12.00 one. For three minutes, the time it takes to run this race, I am totally immersed in the moment. The excitement inside reminds me how, as a child, I wanted to be a jockey. The three of us are following our horses and as they come down the finish line one of my picks, Etheral, is making his move. I am out of my chair and cheering with the rest of the crowd. The jockey is riding her like the wind, she is flat out, she's gaining, and she wins! I am jumping up and down like I have a lot of money riding on her. Like I said, it's exciting to pick the winner. Once the excitement settles I realize I have also picked the third place winner for a grand total win of $32.60. Now if I were a gambler, I would have made some serious money today.

The afternoon is still young so we go out and explore the beaches and cliffs. This is a picturesque place and would be wonderful to roam around for hours, but today is cold and windy. We hike up to one of the lighthouses and walk along the beach, climbing over and around some cliffs. The wind is cold enough to cut our adventure short and force us back to the beach house.

Friday, November 9, I am about to call a cab to take me out to Secon to pick up my bike when I receive a call from Australian Groupage Service. The voice on the line says; "Your bike hasn't arrived."

"What do you mean it hasn't arrived? There must be some mistake—we have the paperwork! I was told the container arrived at Secon on Monday and I could pick it up today."

The AGS informant replies, "The package wasn't on the truck that brought the goods from Sydney to Melbourne."

I am stunned! I can't believe what I am hearing. How could this possibly be? I put down the phone and relay the message to Curtis before taking the train home to figure out what to do next. November is not turning out to be a great month for me. The weather in Melbourne is cool and wet and my missing motorcycle dampens my mood further.

I spend hours on the telephone each morning trying to get information on the whereabouts of my bike. A week later and there is still no sign of it. I have spent the past week on the telephone trying to get answers and neither Australian Groupage Service nor Total Care Trucking Company is able to find the crate. Now, imagine this—a crate almost three meters long, one meter high and two-thirds of a meter wide—wouldn't you think it would be easy to spot? Well, somehow or another, nobody at these two companies can find it. After a week of calling them twice a day, sometimes more, they tell me to submit an insurance claim. Now I am really feeling sick. I do not want to be paid for the bike and have to start looking for another one. I just want my magna back so I can get packed and on the road. Needless to say, I am very upset about all this. My three-month visitor visa is quickly expiring while making phone calls and waiting for people to call me back. Not exactly what I had planned. I am looking into alternate travel plans for the interim—that is until they compensate me for lost goods, or find my bike.

After submitting the insurance claim on Friday, I seek some legal advice from a friend. He suggests that I call AGS and Total Care Trucking again on Monday morning and ask for the names of anyone who handled the crate, and if the bike has been reported to the police as lost or stolen goods.

First thing Monday morning, November 19, I am on the phone again to both companies. Neither company could (or would?) give me names of the people who signed for this shipment. AGS reluctantly gives me a couple of initials and that is all. I insist that they must know whom these initials belong to, but they are not about to tell me. My last request is to ask if they have reported the crate to the police as lost or stolen goods. Both companies reply, "Oh no, we don't do that." I simply cannot believe what I am hearing. I tell them that I will be putting in a report to the police and contacting a lawyer.

One-hour later … **Great news,** they found my bike! My son received a call at work saying the crate has been found. Miraculously it turned up on the dock in Sydney. Now, isn't that interesting? I cannot make accusations because I have no proof, but the whole event has certainly triggered my suspicions.

I pick up my "baby" on Thursday, November 22. All is intact and the bike looking more beautiful than I remembered. Curtis helps me uncrate and reassemble it—put the windshield and mirrors, back on, connect the battery cables, replace oil, fuel, etc. I am so grateful for his help.

Now for my first test of driving on the left side of the road! I am glad to be following Curtis on his bike. I must say, it doesn't feel as strange as I thought it would. I guess riding as a passenger in vehicles over the past month has helped me make the adjustment.

This weekend I will start my journey to the center of Australia. I will travel through New South Wales, South Australia, the Northern Territory, and then back to Melbourne via the Great Ocean road in Victoria.

I am thinking I need a trial run, so on Saturday, Nov. 24 I ride out to Healesville Sanctuary to see the animals, reptiles and birds native to Australia. I'm pleased that I find my way out of Melbourne onto the Maroondah Highway without too much difficulty. The ride is very pleasant and the sun is shining. I soon arrive at the Black Spur nursery and teahouse that was highly recommended by other bikers. Here I stop for lunch and get information on the area before visiting the Sanctuary.

I spend a pleasant afternoon wandering through the Sanctuary. I discover that the koala bear is not a bear at all—no relation what so ever to the bear family; and the small animal that looks like a baby kangaroo is actually a wallaby. The platypus is much smaller than I imagined and darts around in the water very swiftly. Echidnas are covered in a prickly skin and much faster than they look. The flying fox is a giant bat and the 'wombat gully' is not a bat at all, but a very solid, four legged, fury animal. Healesville Sanctuary is home to all kinds of snakes and colorful birds—far too many to remember all their names. I hope to see some of the wildlife in their natural habitat throughout my travels.

Heading back to Melbourne I follow the winding, twisty road through the eucalyptus forest. I take my time and enjoy the smell of the eucalyptus trees. The road is narrow with no shoulder and no room for error. Several sport bikes pass me in a blur and I shudder at the thought of them missing a curve. My guess is they have ridden these roads numerous times and know every corner by heart.

I am back in Melbourne in time to take Curtis and Vanessa out for dinner. They have chosen a Thai restaurant to enjoy our last evening together. Australia is a multicultural country very much like Canada, so good food from all cultures is available. We enjoy a fabulous evening together ... tomorrow I venture out to discover Australia. My plan is to be back in Melbourne for Christmas—that only gives me a month to see half of the country. Once again I am annoyed at the shipping company for losing my bike and delaying my travels by two weeks.

Australia is a huge country with a lot to see. I head north from Melbourne to Bendigo. En route, I take the Mount Macedon turnoff and go through green hillsides with estates, golf courses and resorts on both sides of the road. This is obviously a wealthy area. I continue on to Hanging Rock Park where I stop and hike up to the top of the pinnacles. Huge rocks sit perched above the ground looking like they could topple over if you gave them a slight push. I make it to the top and am rewarded with a panoramic view that compensates for the strenuous climb.

After a few pictures and time to absorb the beauty, I start my descent. I only walk a short distance when I see a koala in a tree eating on the eucalyptus leaves. What a bonus! The path down takes me right under the hanging rock—a huge boulder, suspended by two much bigger boulders protruding out of the ground, creating an arch over the path. This is what gave the park its name.

As I continue on to Bendigo, the weather becomes cold and it looks like rain. The wind picks up, and by the time I reach Bendigo, I am cold and happy to stop. I am not taking a chance on camping tonight so I find a camping cabin for 33 Australian dollars. Many of the campgrounds in Australia have what they call 'camping cabins'—small trailers similar to those used for offices at construction sites. They have a kitchen, small eating area, queen size bed and another room with two double bunk beds—very comfortable and big enough for a whole family.

Next morning the sun is shining and breaking up the patches of clouds. I head over to the visitor centre, then to the Bendigo lookout tower. I marvel at the view from the top of the tower and search out some landmarks with my binoculars. On the pad below I admire the mosaic artwork depicting the history of Bendigo.

I ride out of town around noon, following the old gold route. This is a sightseeing day so I will not be making a lot of kilometers. I ride through farming countryside with fields of grain and pastures of sheep and cattle. I stop at Newbridge to photograph the St. John's Anglican Church—an old brick building built sometime in the 1800's. As I ride across the grassy yard the cows moo at me from across the fence. What a peaceful setting—life is great!

Shortly after 1:00 PM, I reach the quaint little town of Dunolly and find the Dunolly Bakery. The gal inside strikes up a conversation with me, and soon reveals that she has a 500cc Honda, but has not ridden the past few years. Seeing mine makes her yearn to get her bike back on the road. I order a fresh beef and mushroom pastie for $2.50 and an apple turnover for $1.75. This is the best lunch I have had on the road and at the best price—in Melbourne that would have cost ten dollars.

My hunger satisfied, I walk down the street to the public washrooms. That's right, down the street. Not all food outlets have washrooms for their customers. The toilets, not called bathrooms (bathrooms are where you take a bath), are behind the old town hall. I stop to admire the architecture of this building and others across the street, when a journalist stops to tell me about the history of the buildings. Built in the early eighteen hundreds, they are now being developed into museums. When the project is complete they will give tours of the old town. This kind gentleman opens the doors to the old town hall and lets me preview their displays. I feel honoured!

Continuing on the gold route I come to Maryborough, an impeccably maintained, thriving little town, boasting new home construction everywhere. It appears to be a fast growing community. After a few turns and curves I reach Newstead, then Maldon. I stop at Maldon and walk out to the remains of the Beehive Goldmine—just one of the many mines scattered along this route. Back on the road and a few more turns, I find myself completely lost, not knowing what direction I am going. It does not take much to become disoriented when traveling in the southern hemisphere. I notice my bike is running low on fuel so I stop a vehicle to ask for directions so as not to waste fuel riding off into the middle of nowhere. Wouldn't you know it—I left my jerry can back at the cabin. I make it back to Bendigo and lecture myself on taking my jerry can everywhere. Australia is a big country with long distances between fuel stations.

I am adjusting comfortably to riding on the left side of the road. The two most difficult things are turning corners and meeting an oncoming vehicle in a curve. My heart jumps on a few occasions when I think a vehicle is coming right at me.

Over the next couple of days, I cross from Victoria to New South Wales where I make my way north to Broken Hill. This is desert country, *very* hot and *very* dry. I watch attentively for kangaroos but the best I see are the ones lying dead on the side of the road, hit by large trucks traveling at night and in the early mornings. I do happen to spot a pair of emus and manage to get a picture before they run off. The emu is huge, standing over 1.8 meters tall, weighing approximately fifty kilograms, and is Australia's largest bird.

I have been traveling through desert for several kilometers when, nearing Broken Hill, I see what appears to be a big lake off in the distance. I feel excited and pick up speed. Imagine how early settlers would have felt, after traveling for days, weeks, or months by horse or camel through this vast desert, to spot water ahead. I watch the kilometers tick by on my odometer and soon realize there is no water. What a disappointment! I feel discouraged, as if it were crucial that I find water! I think again of how early settlers might have felt. A few more kilometers and I cross over a short bridge with signage saying *Pine Creek*. There is no water here either, just cracked red sand and gnarled trees.

As I approach Broken Hill my first thought is, *there's a cement or brick wall around the town*. As I ride closer I see that the *wall* is built around the hill that is Broken Hill Mine. Lead, iron ore, zinc and silver are mined here. In its peak years the mine employed eight thousand people, now there are four hundred.

Silverton, which is just a few kilometers out of Broken Hill, was once the biggest producing silver mine in the world. The town once had a population of thirty thousand. Today it looks like it would be hard to find fifty people. I stop at the Silverton Hotel and Pub for lunch and a beer. This hotel was used to shoot scenes in the movies; *A Town Like Alice, Mad Max 11, Razor Back* and *Dirty Deed*.

From here I go southwest and cross into South Australia. I camp at Port Augusta one night before heading north towards the center of this great continent. My destination is Coober Pedy to find the opal mines. The scenery along this route becomes quite monotonous with flat open desert, a few bushes and small trees, sagebrush scattered here and there, and red earth. Occasionally some interesting shaped hills pop up out of nowhere. I count the dead 'roos' on the side of the road to break the monotony. About one every ten kilometers! This is no fun. An old song pops into my head; "Keep your mind on your drivin', keep your hands on the wheel. Keep your beady eyes on the road ahead. We're havin' fun, sittin' in the back seat, kissin' and a huggin' with Fred." Anyone who rides knows how these silly, little jingles creep into your head and spin around and around like a broken record until you want to scream—stop, stop, stop!

Over and over these lyrics spin. The wind pushes on my bike reminding me to pay attention. The last stretch traveling to Coober Pedy is 252 kilometers between fuel stations. "No problem," I tell myself. "I can get 260 kilometers out of a tank, plus I have my spare four liters." That is in perfect conditions—traveling at one hundred kilometers per hour, with no wind. Today is not perfect. The wind becomes stronger and stronger the farther inland I travel. My bike is being knocked around fiercely at times. The occasional large vehicle I meet gives me a good blast and sends me to the side of the road. I keep my speed at a hundred, and when my trip meter reads 154 the bike gives a couple of sputters and I switch to reserve. *This is not good!* I watch the signposts, CP90, CP80, (indicating the distance to Coober Pedy) and cut my speed down to eighty. When my trip meter reads 203 kilometers my bike sputters and I coast to the side of the road. Just before running out of fuel I saw a sign "P500m" (parking 500 meters). I silently begged, please, just let me make it to the parking area. No such luck. I run out right in front of the sign "P300m".

Was that lightening I just saw? I un-strap my jerry can of spare fuel and pray I don't spill a drop. Success! With four liters now in my tank I prepare to ride and keep my speed at eighty. The sky is black and lightening dances overhead. Thunder is crashing loudly and the wind blowing harder. I keep watching the distance on the posts at the side of the road (CP30, CP20) and on my trip meter, silently praying, *please get me there*. At last I turn into Coober Pedy and into the first petrol station I see. Wow, I hope I never encounter a situation like that again.

My plan was to camp in their underground campground, but at this point I am just too tired and take a motel instead. The gal behind the desk is very helpful. After checking me in she says, "There's going to be a huge dust storm tonight, maybe you'd like to watch it. This one should be quite spectacular." I cannot believe I am hearing this! I just battled major winds for the past three and a half hours and am not interested in seeing a dust storm.

The people in Coober Pedy are wonderful. After a short rest I make my way to the Gemstone Café and Bakery and order a sandwich and a beer. "Sorry, we don't sell liquor here," says the waiter. "You can go across the road and buy it at the liquor store. I'm not licensed to serve it to you, but if no one sees you bring it in, I'll pour it into a coffee cup for you."

I chuckle at the thought and cannot resist this little bit of naughtiness, so across the road I go and bring back a 6 pack in a brown bag. Dave, who is the waiter and cook, takes the bag and tucks it under the counter. With my sandwich I enjoy a coffee cup of brew.

Dave is a good-looking man, about forty, of average height, reddish blond hair, with a great tan. I strike up a conversation with him about the opal mining in this area. He tells me Coober Pedy is the largest opal producing fields in the world. I ask him if there are mine tours, and he suggests that I not take one of those touristy packages. "Find a miner who will take you down into his mine," he says.

"Well, how am I going to do that?" I ask.

Before I know it Dave is on the phone arranging a tour of a working opal mine with a prospector/miner named Juergen. I can hardly believe my luck.

I am excited about the prospect of going down into a working mine, but as I stroll back to my room I begin to wonder if I am being too trusting by accepting a tour from strangers. I could be raped, or killed and left in a pit and nobody would know. The worrying begins to escalate and I contemplate canceling. I am too tired to think, so I let the thought go. I will see how I feel in the morning and then make a decision.

At 8 o'clock next morning I meet Dave at the restaurant and he drives me to the outskirts of Coober Pedy to meet Juergen. Juergen is a big, rough looking character, unruly dark hair and a beard, with a big friendly smile. He takes me into the cave he is living in. Sixty percent of the population lives in underground homes called caves or dugouts. These caves remain much cooler in the desert heat than traditional homes. Juergen's cave is definitely a male domain and a little rough looking, but has all the comforts of home. Later in the day he takes me to visit some friends of his whom own a beautiful cave. I am impressed!

The walls and ceilings are not smooth or square but have circular ridges created from the huge drilling machines used to dig out the cave. A clear glue-type sealer preserves the natural finish of rock and soil, which ranges in color from sandstone to all shades of pink. The floor is tile, the kitchen cupboards are like those in traditional homes and the layout is open and spacious. The house is built into the side of a huge hill about half way up. A big garage or workshop is built into the hill about a quarter of the way around and lower down. The value of this home (cave) is between $150,000 and $200,000.

For now we are going opal mining. Dave, Juergen and I pile into Juergen's beat up old 1970 *Ute,* which has a winch built into the box. We rumble along rough roads through the mining fields, Juergen pointing out some of the larger mines. He explains that any prospector can purchase a piece of land with the rights to mine it. We reach our destination out in the desert and Dave cautions me to be careful where I walk because there are open mine holes everywhere. Juergen backs the truck up to a hole in the ground that is the entrance to his mine. I am soon to learn that the winch in the box of the truck is our means of descending into the mineshaft.

Dave is lowered down first, and then it is my turn. Juergen gives me a hard hat and hands me the triangular bar (something like a tow bar on a ski hill). He instructs me to position the bar below my butt to support my weight. A thick cable comes from each end of the bar forming a triangle which connects to a long rope attached to the winch. I step inside the triangle and hold onto the cable as I am lowered into the mine. I place my feet against the inner shaft, walking downward about fifteen meters (fifty feet), until I reach the open space of the mine below. Dave helps me get my feet on the ground and I step out of the towrope apparatus, which is pulled up once more for Juergen to descend.

I am amazed at how spacious the drives (tunnels) are. We walk through meters and meters of drives about a meter wide and high enough to stand upright. Juergen warns me not to stand below an open shaft as dirt and debris may fall in. He then goes on to explain what they look for in the walls, pointing out the direction of the grain and the texture of the soil. After a tour of the whole mine he picks a spot to drill. He uses a black light against the wall that exposes the opal unseen by the naked eye. You can hear the crunch from the drill as it goes through gypsum, rock and opal. As the dirt falls under the black light, little pieces of opal shine through. Anything that is worth looking at is put into a big sack and taken back to the workshop and put through a washing process to be cleaned and graded. Before we leave, Juergen turns the drill over to me and I get to try my hand at drilling for opal. What a treat! I would not have experienced that on a guided tour. Ninety percent of the world's opals come from Australia.

We spend about two hours in the mine before gathering up our finds and tools and repeating the winch process to take us back above ground. Coming up is a bit trickier than going down. I am cautioned not to look up as dirt may fall in my eyes. "Just walk your feet along the side of the shaft and Juergen will guide you when you are at the top," Dave says. With everything loaded, the old Ute bounces along as we head back into town. Dave has to go to work, so we drop him off and Juergen becomes my tour guide and shows me the sights of Coober Pedy.

First he gives me a lesson on how to spot the caves. To the unfamiliar eye they are unrecognizable, but once I know what to look for I spot several. Many of them are built into the side of the hills and some are built straight down from level ground. Today Juergen stops at the Serbian Orthodox Church. This church is off limits to visitor tours, but Juergen has work to do here and asks the priest if he can go in to do some measuring. What a brilliant man. We enter the cave to a modest foyer then turn left into the chapel. My first comment is, "There are no pews." Juergen explains that they either stand or sit on the floor to worship. This room is approximately fifteen meters long, nine meters wide and six meters high. The stairs leading up to a balcony at the back houses the baptismal tank, and behind the pulpit is another room, which we do not enter. The walls are like those in the home I described earlier. The varying colors of pink embedded in the circular ridges give it a special feeling all its own.

As we are driving around I comment on all the different clubs they have in Coober Pedy. Juergen says, "Oh yes, we have the Italian Club, Mexican Club, Serbian Club, Croatian Club … we have all kinds of clubs, the United Club, the Lions Club, the Fu*#*… Golf Club" … he finishes with a chuckle. I try hard to stifle my laughter.

Juergen drops me off in town and I promise to buy him dinner and a beer this evening for his gracious hospitality. In the mean time I wander through the Desert Cave Inn, a five star hotel with opal shops, art shops, jewelry shops and much more. I walk to the Big Winch which houses a good quality gift shop and provides the best view of Coober Pedy. From here I find my way back to my motel, shower and get ready for dinner. What a great day this has been!

Leaving Coober Pedy next morning I head north on the Stuart Highway. For the first forty kilometers I am riding through opal fields. Large pyramids of red earth adorn the landscape—some clustered closely together and others scattered farther apart. These piles of earth have been excavated to form hundreds of mines. Back in Port Augusta a fellow camper had commented that all this destruction is due to woman's vanity. I am not sure I agree. Could it be due to man's greed? Just a thought ...

Once past the opal fields the desert becomes green with small desert plants and trees. Usually the temperatures this time of year are over 40°C making everything brown, but this year there has been heavier rainfall than usual and the desert plants are green and flowering. Two hours later I cross into the Northern Territory.

Australia has some unique road signs—many animal signs warning of camel, kangaroo, and wombat, but also precautionary signs. South Australia and the Northern Territory signs read *DROWSY DRIVERS DIE*. Back in New South Wales the typical signs read; *STOP REVIVE SURVIVE*.

As I ride closer to Erldunda the sky looks unsettled again. I notice pools of water lying in the ditches and some debris scattered around. When I reach Erldunda I am told that a storm went through last night, broke tree branches and dumped a lot of water. The campground was quite a mess earlier, but the cleanup crew is doing a good job of putting it back in order.

I fuel up my bike before setting up tent, silently hoping this storm does not come through again tonight. Hundreds of Galahs (grey or white birds with pretty pink feathers on their neck and breasts) fill every branch of the trees, and are squawking loudly. I am thinking I will never sleep tonight if this continues. I organize my gear and go in search of something to eat. Everything is much more expensive here. Being so isolated they can charge what they want because there is nothing else around.

Back at the campground the Galahs are still squawking—the noise is *deafening!* I retrieve my earplugs from the bike. A short time later, at 8:00 PM, the campground is quiet. I look up in the trees, and yes, the Galahs are still there; they have become completely quiet. I ask some local people about this and am told "don't worry, they'll start again in the morning." Sure enough, before 6:00 AM they start singing again.

I am up with the birds, pack up my tent and begin my journey to Uluru in Kata Tjuta National Park. The park is located 450 kilometers southwest of Alice Springs. I stop in Curtain Springs for fuel and breakfast then hit the road again. Today is a short day and I arrive in Yulara (Ayres Rock Resort) before noon. I set up camp before walking to the visitor center for a map of the area and whatever information they can give me.

I ride out to Uluru, more commonly known as Ayres Rock, the world's largest monolith and a sacred site to the Aboriginal people. I stop at the site where visitors are allowed to hike the tough, 1.6-kilometer trail to the top of the rock. I get my hiking boots on, toss my riding jacket across the bike, and head to the base of the Rock. I climb up the first bulge, about 100 meters, then start up the next steeper section. Suddenly I lose my nerve. I stop for a moment then try again. *This is ridiculous, I'm not afraid of heights!* I make a couple more attempts but simply cannot force myself to continue. There are other people climbing ahead of me, I should have no problem, but I cannot make myself go farther. I retrace my steps to the bottom and go back to my bike, not too sure what just happened.

I decide to ride around Uluru and make several stops to hike some trails that lead into the rock. I am about half way around when the clouds start rolling in. Soon rain is pouring down and lightning is flashing across the sky. I think about the people who were climbing Ayres Rock ahead of me and by now would be at the top. Now I know why I could not continue my climb.

At 5:00 AM on December 5 I awake to the sound of zippers from the tents around me. People are getting up early to see the sun rise over Uluru. I poke my head out to a cloudy sky. It had rained most of the night so I am in no hurry to get up. I drift back to sleep for an hour and by 6:00 I am up and start packing. My tent is wet so I shake it out best I can and roll it up. By 7:00 I am ready to go.

Not much is open this early—I think today is Sunday. The only restaurants open are at the Desert Inn and the Outback Pioneer Lodge. Both have buffets priced from $19.95 (continental) to $26.95 (full). I cannot justify paying that much when I don't even feel hungry, so I continue on to the gas station for fuel and settle for a fruit cookie and coffee for $3.80.

The sky is starting to clear as I ride out to Kata Tjuta (the Olgas). The Olgas are a dramatic series of thirty-six dome-like rock formations of various shades of pink and red. They reach up to 546 meters (1,701feet) in height and cover an area of about thirty-five kilometers. I hike for about an hour through the rocks. The sun has come out creating vibrant colors over the red rocks that cast their shadows across the sand. The blue sky and the blue/green eucalyptus trees growing amongst the rocks create a glorious contrast. I am told that sunset is a particularly magical time to visit the park. As the sun sets over the rocks it produces an incredible light show of changing colors.

Back on my bike, I backtrack now towards Curtain Springs for fuel and lunch. I stop at a little restaurant with tables outside under a large straw canopy. It looks like an inviting and interesting place to eat. I order roast beef and gravy on a bun from a gal doing dishes along one side of the dining area. She asks Cookie, who emerges from behind the grill, if that is still available. Cookie is a little five foot nothing man about sixty years old with a beard extending down to his chest.

He mumbles something that I cannot quite hear then turns to me and grumps, "It'll have to be on an un-toasted bun."

"No problem, plain bun is fine," I reply politely, thinking, *Oh dear, toasting the bun is the easy part. I wonder how he'll handle the beef and gravy!*

I pick a table under the canopy and soon Cookie delivers my meal with a smile. Immediately a big dog saunters over and lies by my chair. After a couple of bites another big dog comes from across the yard and plops himself on the other side of my chair. I am almost finished eating, trying hard to ignore them, when I notice a third dog watching me from under the table. As I get up to pay for my lunch, which was delicious, another dog gets up from behind me. Wow! I guess I should have shared ... but I was really hungry.

I gear up and continue on to Kings Creek and Kings Canyon. After about fifty kilometers on the Lasseter Highway I turn north onto Luritja Highway. The countryside is getting hillier and the road has a few curves. Here the desert is very green with more trees than farther south—quite colorful! The green does not come without rain. I encounter a couple of places en route where the road is flooded, so I slow down and cross very carefully. I stop for fuel at Kings Creek then continue on to Kings Canyon. The canyon on my right is cast in sunlight, enhancing the pink and red colors. As I ride past looking for a campground I make a mental note to come back. A short time later I reach Kings Canyon Resort, set up camp, and call it a day. This time I have picked up groceries to make dinner and breakfast. I am getting wise to the high costs of meals out here in the outback.

It rained most of the night so I allow myself to sleep in next morning. At about 7:00 AM I poke my head out of my tent. The sky is clouded over but not raining. I get dressed in my riding gear and ride about ten kilometers to Kings Canyon. As I am shedding my riding gear it starts to sprinkle. Oh well, think of it this way, this is better than hiking in 40°C temperatures. By 7:30 I start the six-kilometer trail in the rain. There are a couple of small tour groups on the trail and I quickly pass them. The climb is exhilarating and by the time I have reached the top, an hour later, the rain has subsided and the sky begins to clear. I walk along the edge of the platforms of rock that overlook the canyon until I reach the highest point, about 250 meters from its base. Cautiously, I walk closer to the edge and peer down with my binoculars. Incredible view!

The trail traverses along the top for awhile longer before starting down into the canyon. Wooden stairs take me down and across a bridge, then more stairs descend to rock pathways that eventually take me back up the other side of the canyon. I look back and marvel at the sight and the fact that I was just standing over there on the opposite cliff. I continue my hike along the canyon ridge, over and around rocks and around bends, following the trail that leads me back to the parking lot and my bike. Three hours to hike Kings Canyon. Wow, what a fantastic sight! I am pleased with myself for having completed this.

There are more big tour buses in the parking lot and I am glad I went early. Once back at the campground I realize my watch is out an hour and the time now is 10:00 AM. I had started my hike at 6:30, not 7:30.

I decide to pack up my tent and ride back to Erldunda, then on to Alice Springs. At Mt. Ebanezer I stop for fuel and a bite to eat. In the few minutes I am inside it begins to pour rain. The black cloud is coming from the same direction I came; the sky is blue to the north where I am going. I decide to continue and soon a dark grey cloud forms to my right. The blue is almost gone. I have only ridden five kilometers in the pouring rain and contemplate turning back, but my brief experience here in the desert has taught me it can change quickly. I continue for another twenty kilometers in the wind and rain, and just as abruptly as the rain started, it quit! The sun has come out and the temperature is rising, drying my gear quickly.

I take a campsite at Erldunda once again and walk to the pub for a beer. I am told that it has been pouring steadily from here to Alice Springs (another two hundred kilometers north) and warned not to continue, especially with my bike. When these roads flood it is difficult and sometimes impossible to get through, even with a 4X4. I decide to wait until morning to make my decision.

I order a light dinner while chatting with a tall, strapping young man. He has been working in the mines and has a couple of days off. The distance home is too far so he will spend his time off in Erldunda. He asks where I have been and if I am enjoying myself. I talk about Ayres Rock and Kings Canyon. He chuckles and says, in his thick Australian accent, "It's just a rock. We have all kinds of them sticking up all over Australia, they're just rocks." It is quite obvious he thinks us *tourists* are amused by simple things.

Alice Springs is in the centre of the Australian outback. The Stuart Highway and the Great Transcontinental Railway connect it to the north and south. The railway connects to the east/west track at Tarcoola, South Australia, and ends at Alice Springs. I would really like to ride to Alice Springs and continue north across this great continent.

The rain continues all evening. Around 11:00 PM I awake to thunder and lightning, and the rain coming down in buckets. I check my tent—miraculously the inside is still dry. The thunder cracks and rolls across the sky for an hour with barely a pause between the end of one and the beginning of the next. Lightning illuminates the sky and my tent. No need for a flashlight tonight. Just as I thought it couldn't rain any harder the thunder gives a series of extra loud crashes and the rain pours harder. Sometime through the night it stops, but by 6:30 AM, just as I have finished packing up, it starts again.

Today is December 7, 2001. I decide to forgo my plan of riding to Alice Springs, Katherine, Broome and around the west coast to Perth. Instead I will retrace my route south towards Coober Pedy and hope to reach Glendambo today. I do not relish the thought of riding the 252-kilometer stretch between Coober Pedy and Glendambo again. Oh well, it simply cannot be helped.

Rains are hitting the north much harder than usual this year. Water is lying in puddles on the road and the ditches are full. The rain has made the desert green and flowers are popping out all over. Little pink flowers cover the ground in large patches and the few trees I see are green.

I reach Coober Pedy in the early afternoon and stop at the Gemstone Café for lunch. Dave is working and I have a nice visit with him before continuing on to Glendambo. As I fear, this stretch is windy again and I use my spare fuel before reaching my destination. I have traveled 733 kilometers today and don't feel like putting up camp, so I treat myself to a bunkhouse with a bed and bathroom for $15.50.

I am on the road early next morning and reach Port Augusta before noon. A couple of days to travel the great ocean road and I'll be back in Melbourne. I told Curtis and Vanessa I would be back for Christmas, but that is still over two weeks away, so I decide to ride farther west to see more of Australia.

The sun is shining but the air is cool. I stop for fuel out of necessity and for a chance to warm up. At Pimba I get toast and coffee for $3.70—prices start to come down as I ride back into more populated areas.

From Port Augusta I take Alt. highway A1, which takes me on the coastal route of the Eyre Peninsula, stopping in at some lovely towns tucked in bays along the waters edge of Spencer Gulf. After 600 kilometers I find a campground at Tumby Bay, set up camp, and go for a walkabout. The ride today has been quite enjoyable with gentle curves and stunning scenery all around me. There is just something about being near the water that adds a therapeutic feel to the air.

Next morning I continue my route on Alt. A1 stopping at Port Lincoln and Coffin Bay. My wild imagination saw thousands of people buried here due to some disaster. Not so, Coffin Bay is known as one of Australia's great boating, windsurfing and fishing areas. Matthew Flinders named it in 1802 in honour of Sir Isaac Coffin.

I make stops at Elliston, Venus Bay and Streaky Bay before stopping at Ceduna to camp. Today I have come past farmland with wheat fields swaying in the breeze; pasture land housing sheep and cattle, water on my left and small mountain ranges off in the distance to my right, creating a mystery of life on the other side. It has truly been a wonderful day. I have only ridden 500 kilometers today, but I stop early at Ceduna so I can catch up on e-mails to family and friends.

December 10 I head west across the Nullarbor Plains on the Eyre Highway, A1, leaving South Australia behind. There is not much to see from the highway so I take a couple of short rides off to the south to see the Great Australian Bight. I walk around at the Head of Bight wishing it were whale-watching season. Head of Bight is famous for its whale watching from May to October. I stop at Bunda Cliffs and soak in the view of the majestic cliffs that drop straight down creating a solid wall against the ocean. Continuing on I stop at a little place called Border Village that marks the boundary between South and Western Australia. Somewhere along this stretch I saw a sign that read *East end of a treeless plain*. I am soon to find out how true that is!

At Cocklebiddy I find a motel and take a room. I have ridden 780 kilometers and crossed over half the Nullarbor Plains. I am ready for a rest. Service stations are called Roadhouses, and out here in the middle of nowhere the price of fuel escalates once again. The roads are dotted with dead kangaroo. Road signs warn "Camel, Kangaroo, Wombat" or "Camel, Roos, Emus."

Next morning I leave Cocklebiddy at 6:30 and arrive in Caiguna forty-five minutes later—still 6:30. I have gained forty-five minutes crossing a time zone. The Eyre Highway parallels (although far from sight) the infamous Transcontinental Railway that runs east and west across Australia, connecting Sydney on the east coast to Perth on the west. The road is long and straight, one section boasting the longest straight stretch of road in Australia (possibly the world). That stretch is 146.6 kilometers, or ninety miles, without so much as a bend and only a slight degree of horizontal change. I park my bike under the sign and take a picture, set my trip meter to zero and continue, holding the throttle at a steady one hundred and forty kilometers per hour. I keep a constant eye out for camels, roos and emus but do not see any for miles, except for dead roos. I notice that most of the vehicles have a steel grill guard mounted on the front of their vehicles. A short time later I see six or eight roos bound across the highway in the distance. Later I see two emus in the ditch on my left, soon four more on my right. No camels though.

I glance down at my trip meter ... 144kms. I look ahead in the distance. Is that it? Yes, I think I see it—145 kilometers, now I am sure of it. The excitement builds ... 146 kilometers and I am there, leaning into the first, ever so gentle curve in 146.6 kilometers! I have just ridden the longest straight stretch in the world in just over an hour.

A brief stop for fuel then I continue the last two hundred kilometer ride on the Eyre Highway to Norseman, where I stop for lunch and more fuel. Over lunch I visit with a couple of fellows from Holland who are traveling by jeep around Australia. Meeting people from other parts of the world, with the same adventurous spirit, is a real treat. There is something to be learned from each and every one.

Fueled and fed up, I continue on to the gold mining town of Kalgoorlie-Boulder. I check into the VIP backpacker hostel—very clean and comfortable with all the amenities needed. I have met some interesting people in hostels and it always impresses me what good cooks a lot of the young men are. Then I realize that it is the mothers of my generation who have taught them. Ladies, we have done a good job!

Kalgoorlie still has a red light district. One block down from the hostel is a whole block of brothels, that I am told are still legally in operation. One of them has been made into a museum as a tourist attraction. These Aussies sure know how to capitalize on the tourist industry.

Boulder is home of the *Super Pit*—Australia's largest open-cut gold mine and one of the largest mesozonal gold deposits in the world. The *Pit* extends 3.5 kilometers in length, 1.5 kilometers across and is approaching four hundred meters deep.

In June of 1893, prospectors Paddy Hannon, Tom Flanagan, and Dan O'Shea stumbled upon gold during their travels to Mt. Youle. Hannon filed a Reward Claim on June 17th of that same year, resulting in hundreds of men swarming the area in search of gold, and Kalgoorlie was born. Concentrated areas of gold and other metals were found between Kalgoorlie and Boulder, which soon became known as the "Golden Mile". This stretch was claimed by some to be the richest square mile of earth on the planet. In 1989 the town of Kalgoorlie and the shire of Boulder amalgamated to become the city of Kalgoorlie-Boulder. The town's population in 1903 was about thirty thousand. Today it is approximately twenty-eight thousand.

There is a lot to see and do in this historic city. I schedule my day to fit in as much as possible. I visit one of the museums in town, and then ride up to the Super Pit … what an amazing view! My next visit is the Gold Miners Hall of Fame that includes a tour of a Gold Mine. We are outfitted with safety vests and hard hats before being loaded (or should I say squeezed), five people at a time, into a small square elevator box, which is lowered forty meters down the mine shaft. Once we reach the bottom we off-load into narrow drives tall enough to stand. These drives are not spacious like the opal mines in Coober Pedy. We are warned to watch our heads and our step as we are led through the dark tunnels. I am happy to return to surface. I don't believe I could handle being that closed in for any length of time.

I am fortunate to be in Boulder on Wednesday. The Boulder Town Hall houses a priceless piece of art painted by the renowned artist, Phillip Goatcher. Discovered by accident in the historic hall, it is the world's last surviving example of a working stage curtain—the scene depicting the Bay of Naples. The Curtain has hung in the Boulder Town Hall since it's opening in 1908. On Wednesdays and Boulder Market days The Curtain is dropped by its original pulley system and open for public viewing. I feel so fortunate to have the opportunity to view this great piece of art.

Just before sunset I ride a few kilometers out of town to see the life size sandstone sculptures erected in the desert. I take my time hiking the trail through the park, stopping to enjoy these wonderful pieces of art, and marvel at the changing shades of color created by the setting sun.

In the morning I go west on Highway 94 to Merredin, then south to Hyden to view the Wave Rock. This unique formation is a granite cliff fifteen meters high and one hundred and ten meters long. Its wave-like shape has been created from water and wind erosion that has undercut the base and left a rounded overhang. Water from the springs run down the rock, dissolving minerals adding color to the rock. Aborigines were the first to inhabit the area but the belief is they stayed clear of the rock for fear of the spirit of Mulka. A short distance from here is Mulka's Caves.

I take the time to hike under the mammoth wave, constantly aware of the massive weight of rock that hangs over me. I walk the length of the wave under the cliff before climbing to the top and hiking the ridge, then following the path up the hill. Upon return I ride the short distance to Mulka's Caves and try to envision the people who once lived here.

When I return to my bike I am completely disoriented. I start to ride but am not sure which direction to go to get back to Hyden. I flag down a passing car and ask for directions. I am amazed once again at how easy it is to become disoriented.

From Hyden I make my way to Corrigan, past farming country with wheat fields blowing in the breeze, and find a Caravan Park. Today, having traveled 745 kilometers, I am ready to set up camp. Jenny, at check in, is extremely helpful and tells me that stores will be closing soon so if I want groceries I should go right away. I off load my gear and Jenny comes over and offers me a ride to the grocery store. She drives me to a place she usually shops and I buy groceries for dinner tonight. Before going back to the campground she takes me on a short tour of the town—what great hospitality.

The wind has come up again and it tugs at my tent as I set up. The Caravan Park has a little cookhouse where I make dinner, protected from the wind. The wind seems to be getting stronger—I hope my tent doesn't blow away tonight.

I make it through the night without windburn, saddle up and am ready to ride at 6:30 AM. The temperature is cold this morning and I wear my fleecy vest and jean jacket under my riding jacket. I left my heated liner at my son's in Melbourne, thinking that I would not need it this time of year in Australia. That was a mistake!

I decide to cut across country today taking the Brookton highway west and turning north just before the Avon River. I follow the Avon River north to the little town of York. The Avon Valley is a lovely route through farmland of wheat fields, rolling hills, curvy roads and interesting little towns. I think this is some of the prettiest country I have seen so far. York, as noted by the Heritage Society of Australia, is Western Australia's most historically rich town. Nestled on the banks of the Avon River, it boasts Victorian and Federation buildings that have been meticulously restored. I stop and do a walkabout before settling on an interesting little café for a scone and cappuccino. A freelance writer for the local paper stops and chats for awhile. I wonder if he will do an article about my trip for his paper.

I contemplate staying here a day and checking out the area more extensively, but today is December 14 and I have not reached Perth yet. I will never make it back to Melbourne by Christmas. I shed my jean jacket and vest from under my riding jacket before continuing on to

New Norcia. The countryside is gorgeous. The road follows the curve of the river and is lined with lush green hills and valleys.

New Norcia is a little town that was started in 1848 by two Spanish Benedictine Monks. It is Australia's only monastic town, and one of the countries most important heritage sites. I stop for an hour and do a walkabout of this peaceful little town. For 160 years Benedictine monks have lived a simple and quiet life here. Located two hours north of Perth, it still remains a quiet, peaceful little place boasting seven hundred thousand visitors each year.

I have lunch before continuing on, and reach Cervantes mid afternoon. I set up camp in the wind and go in search of information about the Pinnacles in Nambung National Park. I am told the best time to view them is at sunset so I go back to my tent, map in hand, and take a short nap. At about 7:00 PM I ride out to the park to be there before sunset. No one told me I would be riding on sand roads to get to the Pinnacles Desert. Oh well, I am here now—no point in chickening out because of a little sand.

The Nambung National Park in Western Australia is located 250 kilometers north of Perth. Right in the heart of the park is where *Pinnacles Desert* can be seen. Thousands of jagged, sharp-edged columns of limestone pillars rise out of the burnt orange colored sand. They are the fossilized roots of long-dead trees and shrubs. Limestone formed around the roots of plants growing on stable dunes about thirty thousand years ago. The plants died and the dunes moved on, leaving the calcified structures exposed.

After riding over six kilometers of sand, gravel, rocks, potholes and washboard I finally reach this massive field of pinnacles ranging in height from a few centimeters to three and a half meters. I am pleasantly surprised at the vast field of shapes and sizes looking much like the work of a sculptor. I follow the sand road winding its way through the field to a viewpoint where I can watch the sun light up the formations. It is amazing to watch the pinnacles transform in color and cast their shadows as the sun slips behind the hills. Definitely worth the price of admission and the painful six-kilometer ride (twice).

Next morning I continue on to Perth, resisting the temptation to pull off the highway and spend a day or two at one of these inviting beaches along the way. I am really wondering if I could become a full time traveler and stay as long as I want whenever I want. I guess I could be a beach bum here.

Okay, back to reality. I have some bike maintenance to take care of so that is priority on my agenda once I reach Perth. I don't spend a lot of time in the big city; instead decide to ride to Fremantle, which is on the west coast, just a short distance south of Perth. Once again I find myself riding in circles and, when I finally admit I am lost, discover I have gone north of Perth instead of south! I arrive in Scarborough and decide to stay and enjoy the beaches in the morning.

Up early, I spend a leisurely morning at breakfast, and then wash my bike before starting out for the day. Seems like I'm in no hurry to go through Perth again and get lost. I stop at City Beach and do an hour walk on the sand bordering the Indian Ocean. The day is glorious and I decide to sit on the beach awhile—might as well get a bit of a suntan. Half an hour is all I can take. I can feel my shoulders burning so decide to gear up and continue to ride.

Today I reach Fremantle and stop to enjoy the atmosphere of this historic, little, seaport town. I enjoy lunch sitting under an umbrella at an outdoor shopping plaza. Shops line the pedestrian only street lively with street performers. I relax for over an hour, enjoying the music and watching people, before walking through the streets to see more of the old buildings. Fremantle is one of those places you could spend the day sitting around outdoor cafes enjoying coffee and the company of good friends.

Before I leave Fremantle I call Wayne and Hazel Miller from my *Gold Book.* Wayne and Hazel live in Bunbury and invite me to spend the night at their home. For most of the ride the ocean is out of sight, until the last fifteen-kilometers when the landscape changes to one of beauty.

I meet Wayne and Hazel at the information centre and follow them to their home. They are members of the Gold Wing Road Riders Association and the Ulysses Club. The Ulysses Club motto is *Grow Old Disgracefully.* I like that! These wonderful people show me around their town—them on their red 1500cc Goldwing and me following on my magna. For a moment I miss my old bike—that is exactly what I rode before purchasing the magna. I cherish these times riding with fellow bikers.

I take the next five days to travel around this part of the south coast. I tour the Jewel Cave of stalagmites and stalactites just north of Albany. The Jewel Cave is home to one of the longest straw stalactites found in any tourist cave. I feel a bit claustrophobic descending into the cave but once down into the open cavity the beauty of the formations resolves that fear. This cave is one of many to be found in this area along Caves Road. I do not take the time to explore them all and am well rewarded in choosing the Jewel Cave.

I ride out to Cape Leeuwin on the point of Flinders Bay. The wind is strong along the coast and rain begins to fall. On to Pemberton my route takes me through forests of stately tuart trees (a species of eucalyptus) mingled with peppermint trees. The smell of the peppermint and eucalyptus is enhanced by the light rain and reminds me to be thankful for the rainy weather. I stop early this evening, after riding an hour in the rain, and catch up on e-mails and newsletters.

Many of the towns in this area have names ending in 'up'— Yallingup, Onindalup, Nannup, Metricup, et cetera. The word *up* means *water* in the Aboriginal language.

Next morning I awake to a sunny day and a ride through the Karri forest. The smooth barked karri tree (eucalyptus diversicolor) is the tallest tree in Western Australia, growing up to ninety meters high and is prominent in several national parks in the southwest. The Gloucester Tree and the Tree-Top Walk, both popular tourist spots, are located here in Western Australia. I stop at the Gloucester Tree with full intentions of climbing it to the top. Steel pegs have been drilled into it forming a staircase to the top for that exact purpose—climbing it.

I pay my entry fee and look for the toilets before attempting my climb. The park toilets are clean and flush operating, much like we have in our homes. I do my thing and as I am standing there zipping up my pants I hear a *plop* sound behind me. I turn around and there is a *huge* toad in the toilet bowl. *Oh my gosh!* He must have been under the rim when I was sitting there. Good thing I didn't have to sit too long. Later I am to learn that Australia is full of giant sized poisonous toads. You can bet I will look under every rim before I sit in the future.

Okay, enough of that. I am out to climb the sixty-one-meter Gloucester tree. I make it about a quarter of the way before deciding to retreat. My arms do not have the strength it takes to continue. I do a short walk along one of the park trails before riding to Bettleup Falls then on to Walpole.

At Walpole I ride the hilltop route overlooking the inlets and the giant karri and tingle trees, then stop to do the treetop walk. This walk is a suspension bridge built amongst the tops of the ancient empire of giant karri and tingle trees. Its highest section is forty meters, offering an amazing view. What an exhilarating feeling being up that high overlooking this lush green forest.

I continue on to Denmark where I drop my bike turning in sand and gravel. No worries, I am fine, only a broken right mirror on the bike. I will get that replaced in Albany. There are many picturesque places to stop along the Southern Ocean—Albany and Esperance being two of the bigger places.

Today is December 21. I enjoy the ride from Albany to Esperence through farmland, forests, hills and small mountains in the distance. The road is smooth with gentle curves to provide an enjoyable ride. I pass by a eucalyptus tree farm and soak up the scent from the trees. Once I arrive in Esperence I contact Steve and Merle, friends of the Millers from Bunbury and owners of a B&B. Steve and Merle are also bikers and members of the Ulysses Club. They give me a discount rate for a room at their B&B and that evening we have fun exchanging bike stories.

On my way out of Esperence in the morning I take the scenic ocean drive before heading back toward the Nullarbor. I stop at Norseman for fuel and a certificate stating that I have crossed the Nullarbor. After eight hundred kilometers of straight, boring road I stop at Madura for the night. I have lost three quarters of an hour crossing a time zone. The motel I get is awful, probably the worst I have been in. The bed covers are stained and the floor looks like it has not been vacuumed in a week. I decide to bring in my sleeping bag and lay it out on the bed to sleep in. For sixty dollars, I am quite tore up.

December 23 is another long day. I have crossed back into South Australia and, after 873 kilometers, reach Wudinna at 7:00 PM. I have crossed the Nullarbor in two days, gone through two time changes, and am happy to be back in farming country with interesting scenery. I set up camp in Wudinna before finding a tourist information building and booking a cabin for December 24 and 25 at Port Pirie Beach. I do not want to be scrambling for a place to stay on Christmas Eve and Christmas Day. I phone Curtis and Vanessa and let them know that I won't make it back for Christmas.

This is my first Christmas away from my family. I am surprised that I don't feel homesick. I prepare a smashing dinner of shrimp, crab, veggies and rice accompanied with a bottle of Australian Shiraz—simply delicious and a great change from turkey.

After dinner I go for a walkabout in the park and along the beach. The sun is shining, there is no snow, and I am hard pressed to feel that this is Christmas. The only indication of this holiday is the excited, happy children riding their new bicycles around the campground.

I spend two very relaxing days here and on December 26 I continue on to Adelaide and across the Fleurieu Peninsula to Victor Harbor. The Fleurieu Peninsula is exceptionally stunning with rolling hills, trees, farms (which I learn are called blocks), vineyards and winding roads. I enjoy picture perfect views as I round the curves and roll over the crests of hills. In Victor Harbor I book two nights to enjoy the sights along with thousands of other vacationers. It is the summer school break in Australia, running from just before Christmas until the end of February.

While in Victor Harbor I do a walking tour of Granite Island, an uninhabited little island next to Victor Harbor, accessible by walking about half a kilometer across the bridge or taking an historical horse drawn coach. Granite Island is a popular tourist attraction, particularly for people wishing to see the Little Penguins (Fairy Penguin) that breed and live on the island. These penguins are seldom seen during the day, so I join a late evening walking tour and am fortunate to see about a dozen of the little guys. Penguins are amazing creatures—these are particularly fascinating because of their size. They weigh about one kilogram (2.2 pounds) and stand approximately thirty to forty-three centimeters (twelve to sixteen inches) high.

December 28 I reach the Great Ocean road and have a pleasant ride, stopping for pictures at the many great sights along the ocean. The rock formations in the ocean, known as the Twelve Apostles, are just one such stop. Accommodations are almost impossible to get along the coast this time of year and I have trouble finding a room or camp spot the night of December 30. I practically beg for a camping spot, and finally find a caravan park at Anglesea where I put up my tent amongst dozens of others and settle in for the night. Next day I reach Queenscliff where I spend New Years Eve and Day with Curtis, Vanessa and her family. The weather is not great but nor is it bad—with clouds, sun, periodic showers and gentle ocean breezes. We enjoy a wonderful New Years Eve dinner of crayfish, prawns and all the fixings, complimented with champagne and wine. What a wonderful way to end an exciting year—with family and newfound friends.

New Years day I make several phone calls back home to my family. I am excited to talk to them all and hear about their Christmas and New Year. They all wish me well on my travels and wonder how much longer I will be gone.

What a great year I have had, and my journey has just begun! **Year 2002 ... where will it lead?**

****

January 1, 2002, I have been away from home for five months. Am I getting tired of traveling? Am I getting lonely or homesick? Well, with the risk of sounding selfish or cold, the answer is NO! My thirst for adventure and to see the world has just amplified over the past five months. I am ready to see more, experience more, and meet more people—the journey has just begun.

I book a flight for New Zealand leaving January 22, so I have a few days to visit places around Melbourne. One particularly interesting three-day ride is to Portsea and Phillip Island. I follow the Neapean Highway around Port Phillip Bay to Sorrento then Portsea, situated at the tip of the Mornington Peninsula. Portsea is the end of the road and home to million dollar mansions owned by Melbourne's rich and famous, many inhabited only on weekends and holidays. The town faces over the calm waters of Port Phillip Bay on one side and surfing beaches on the ocean side. From here I follow the highway bordering Western Port to Phillip Island. Right in the middle of Western Port is French Island National Park accessible only by ferry, barge or plane.

Once on Phillip Island I follow the signs to the Grand Prix Racetrack. I pay my entry fee to tour the museum, grounds and bleachers and cannot resist asking the clerk if I can take my motorcycle out on the track. Well ... she looks at me kind of strangely and says, "No, there are insurance regulations that don't permit us to let you onto the track." I get the feeling that this is not an uncommon request. I enjoy the museum and marvelous garden trails leading out to the bleachers, but most of all I enjoy sitting in the bleachers enjoying the incredible view of the famous race track overlooking hills, cliffs, beach and ocean. I sit for awhile visualizing myself leaning into the curves, cresting the hills just to lean harder into the next tight curve. It would be a real treat to watch a race from here.

I pull myself away from my daydreams and walk back to my bike. From here I ride out to Deal Rock to view the largest colony of Australian fur seals in the world. What an awe-inspiring experience witnessing thousands of fur seals basking on the rocks in their natural environment from the water.

Day three of this short little excursion, I am up early and have breakfast at Pino's Trattoria. This is worth a mention because it is the first restaurant I have been able to get good pancakes for breakfast since I left Canada. They cater to the Grand Prix Racing circuit and have excellent food.

I leave Phillip Island traveling east along the coast towards Wonthaggi, then Venus Bay, before heading north. The feeling of serenity engulfs me as I ride across the hills through farming country. At one point I stop at the top of a high range of hills and marvel at this beautiful, vast countryside. I can just imagine the feeling of pride these farmers have when they look out over the hills and watch their cattle graze. A peaceful feeling washes over me and I find myself reluctant to leave it behind and return to the city.

Back in Melbourne I have a couple of days to shop for last minute backpacking gear before flying off to Christchurch, New Zealand. I will not be taking my motorcycle—hope I'm not sorry later for this decision. I may rent a car, take a bus, or hitchhike.

Chapter 4

New Zealand — South Island

January 22, I leave Australia to fly to New Zealand with a backpack instead of my bike. My flight on Air New Zealand is comfortable until landing. Landing is very rough as we go through a couple of layers of cloud cover. Once I have cleared customs I arrange for a car rental (which I cannot get until tomorrow) then catch the bus to the Square in Christchurch. I swing my large backpack onto my back and the small one in front, and then start walking to the hostel I pre-booked. Wow, this is heavier than I thought! I might have to cut down on my pack.

After the first day on the south island I know I have made a big mistake not bringing my motorbike. This place is made for biking. How could I have been so foolish? Oh well, now I must make the most of my decision. I am here in Christchurch, New Zealand and will become a backpacker and *tramper* (hiker).

The old car I rent for twenty-nine dollars a day is delivered to the hostel. The rental agent accompanies me for a short drive, to make sure I can drive on the left, before handing over the keys. The steering wheel is on the right and all the controls are opposite to what I am used to. My biggest difficulty is using the signal lights—every time I signal, the windshield wipers flap and water sprays the windshield. That is going to take some getting used to. My new friend, Evelyn, from Perth, kindly offers to come with me for a short drive to read the map so I can concentrate on driving. This is great! Evelyn, who is about my age and an avid traveler, navigates so I don't have to worry about reading signposts and wondering where to turn. We do a little tour of Christchurch and area before returning to the hostel. The morning is still young so I check out, throw my pack into the boot, and go in search of tramping tracks.

I leave Christchurch going west on Highway 73 to Arthur's Pass. I am catching on quickly to the gearshift being on the left. About one hundred kilometers down the road I feel the bump, bump, bump of a flat tire. I call Joe at A1 rentals and he calls roadside service. This tire is not in good shape and I am wondering why it was not changed before they rented the car to me. The total bill for a new tire installed is $66.00. I argue with Joe about the bill and he agrees to pay two thirds of it. He will reimburse $44.00 on the rental bill when I return the car.

The roads are narrow and wind their way around mountains and hills. I am driving across the Island to the west coast, which will take me over the Southern Alps via Arthur's Pass and the Otira viaduct. The viaduct replaces a section of road that was originally built in 1865 to connect Christchurch on the east coast to Greymouth on the west. A thousand men built the original pass with axes, picks, shovels, crowbars and wheelbarrows, rock drills and explosives, and completed it in less than a year. Over a hundred years later, between January 1998 and November 1999, this new Otira viaduct I am traveling on was constructed. This area of the Southern Alps is subject to rock-fall, landslides and winter avalanches, so the viaduct was built thirty-five meters up and out of the way of nature's rumblings. It spans 440 meters, appearing to hang off the side of the mountain!

Skiing, hiking and mountain climbing are popular in Arthur's Pass National Park. Mt Rolleston, at 2,275 meters near the summit of Arthur's Pass, is a favorite for the novice mountain climber.

I find a backpackers lodge owned by Canadians Jill and Larry, and get a bed for the night. It has been an interesting day of driving and sightseeing. Many times I longed for my motorcycle, especially when I met one on the road. But I will not let this keep me from enjoying New Zealand. Already I can see how picturesque this Island is, and I have only traveled half a day.

Next morning I continue on to Greymouth. The east coast of the south island is a dramatic coastline that borders the Tasman Sea. I drive north on highway 6 to find the Pancake Rocks—flat rock formations along the coast formed layer, upon layer, upon layer, looking very much like huge stacks of pancakes.

At one visitor center I ask about the constant hum all around us ... *everywhere!* The information clerk tells me it is the sound of cicadas. These little flying insects are like a grasshopper with wings. The monotonous hum that never stops is accompanied by the clacking of their wings. It becomes background noise for the occasional chirp or trill of a bird. The clerk I speak to assures me they get so used to the noise that they don't even hear it. I can't possibly imagine.

I continue south of Greymouth to Franz Josef where I book into a youth hostel. I do the glacier walk before dusk falls upon us, and then make dinner before preparing for a night hike with two of the youth hostel employees. Once night falls they take some of the hostel guests on a trek in the bush to see the glowworms. I am skeptical but, sure enough, there they are. They light up the underbrush like tiny little Christmas lights.

January 26, my plan is to make Queenstown today. I stop at Fox Glacier and do a hike around Lake Matheson. The tramping trail is good and the views of Mt. Cook in the distance are stunning. This landscape is just so spectacular I want to stop every few kilometers to take pictures. The mountain roads today are very narrow with plenty of tight curves. I ache for my motorcycle. I stop a couple more times and do short hikes—Ship Creek is one such stop. I walk onto the beach where the waves are strong and high, being careful not to go out too far. I only get my feet wet.

At Wanaka I take the Cardrona Valley route and just out of town stop to pick up a hitchhiker. At home I would never do this, but today it feels perfectly normal and safe. Jon is from Switzerland and is hitchhiking his way around New Zealand. He is a tall, dark-haired young man in very good shape. Having company and someone to talk to while I travel is a welcome change.

The Cardrona Valley route takes us along the top edge of a canyon overlooking a vast valley. The narrow, twisty road is sometimes scary as I maneuver one tight hairpin turn after another. Jon does not talk much. I am not sure if my driving or the road is scaring him, or if he is just normally quiet. After an hour of twisty road and great scenery we make our way down towards Queenstown, which is set in a picture-perfect spot built around Lake Wakatipu. I drop my guest off on the main street and go in search of a backpacker's hostel.

Back in Melbourne I had read about the "Servas for Peace" organization—a non-profit organization of travelers around the world who host other travelers. This organization was started in 1947 by a young university student in Switzerland and has grown to become International. I am thinking that this is a good time to follow up on the information given to me and see where it leads. I make a call to the New Zealand secretary, Bert Upjohn, and make an appointment to see him when I return to Christchurch.

Queenstown is a popular place with many tourists walking the streets. I am already wishing I had planned six months to travel through both islands instead of seven weeks. There is so much to see here. I take a drive to Arrowtown, then up to Coronet Peak, the South Islands oldest and most developed ski area that overlooks Queenstown and Wapatipu Lake. The Skippers Canyon road looks very rough and narrow with sharp drop-offs, so I decide not to take it. Can't believe I am such a chicken!

That afternoon I drive to Te Anau and once again pick up a hitchhiker. This time a young lady from Germany, carrying a backpack so big I am thinking she will fall over. The pack is as big as she is. Heidi, a very tiny young lady, is tramping her way around New Zealand and today is on her way to Te Anau to do some multi-day tramps.

I check into a youth hostel then do a walkabout before settling in for the evening. I inquire about the Milford Sound and Doubtful Sound cruises, and am able to book a spot on the Doubtful Sound cruise tomorrow. What luck! This is a two-day cruise through the fiords from Manapouri to the Tasman Sea. Doubtful Sound is the deepest of all the fiords at 420 meters and the second longest at forty kilometers, with three distinct arms going off from it.

January 28 I am up early to prepare for my cruise. After breakfast I pick up some seasickness capsules just to be safe—I wouldn't want to ruin this trip by being sick. Then I find some food to take along for lunch before driving to Pearl Harbor at Manapouri.

I am one of about 50 people boarding the Fiorland Flyer, a double-decker sightseeing boat, to be transported across Lake Manapouri. This is the first leg of our excursion. Once across the lake we are loaded onto two buses that take us over Wilmot Pass at an elevation of about 680 meters. The road is narrow and rough with steep cliffs. The views are spectacular and well worth the uncomfortable bus ride. In about an hour we reach the water again, the beginning of Doubtful Sound, and transfer to the Fiordland Navigator. This is a cruise ship, much bigger than the Flyer, with all amenities including berths.

The Fiorland Navigator takes us to Deep Cove, Malaspina Reach, Doubtful Sound, Shelter Island and finally the Tasman Sea. We are told that the weather in the fiords is often rainy or drizzling, but today the sun is shining producing a picture perfect day. Cruising over the water between cliffs that reach up to nine hundred meters on either side of us and forests untouched by man is exhilarating. We stop to take pictures of the waterfalls cascading down the rocks over six hundred meters into the fiord. There is no end to splendid photo spots.

When we reach the Tasman Sea the captain announces that we are sailing out to sea to view Hares Ear. This is not always possible if the weather does not cooperate. Hares Ear is a little island out in the ocean and home of a fur seal colony. The captain anchors the boat momentarily so we can get pictures, then makes a turn and sails back into the fiords. He moors the ship at *Turning Point of Crooked Arm.* I love the names given to places in New Zealand. The ship has stopped early enough so we can do some kayaking before dinner.

Kayaking is a real treat for me but I am very nervous. I have never been in a kayak before and have visions of rolling over and drowning. The guides on board are wonderful and assure me I will be okay. A guide helps me into the kayak, offers a few instructions, and sends me off bringing up the tail end of the group. The *very* tail end—I am a long way behind. I catch on quickly to the rowing rhythm and, being a person who does not like to be last, work extra hard to catch up. My arms ache, but by the time the group has reached their destination in the water I have overcome half of them. After a very short rest we turn the kayaks back to the ship where a delicious meal is awaiting us.

I sleep like a baby in my little bunk and am up at 6:00 AM so as not to miss the small-boat ride out to the peninsula to view the flora. This time we do not have to paddle, just enjoy the ride. A half hour later we reach the peninsula and are climbing over very slippery rocks to take pictures of the flowers and trees. The sand flies are horrendous and would surely make life miserable for anyone staying out here too long. We are blessed with the presence of a crested penguin. "Crested penguins are not usually seen here," our guide relays.

We boat back to the ship and enjoy a wonderful breakfast, then more breathtaking scenery as we begin our sail back. A bottlenose dolphin joins us, swimming along side the bow of the ship. She keeps pace with us for several minutes before making an abrupt turn and swimming away. I cannot believe I am taking more pictures! "Didn't I just shoot all this yesterday?" The scenery is just so amazing I keep on snapping.

We board a bus once again to cross the Wilmot Pass. I sleep during part of the bus ride before catching the Fiorland Flyer to complete this great adventure. What a wonderful cruise. Besides all the beauty and fun, I have met people from England and Hong Kong who invite me to call on them when I am in their country. How great is that!

Back on land I drive north on Highway 94, a very scenic, narrow and twisty road to Milford Sound. At one place en route I enter a narrow tunnel just to be forced to back out about half a kilometer to allow a big bus to pass through from the opposite direction. Milford Sound is another popular tourist area for tramping and cruising through the fiords. I am only doing the drive to see the countryside. I would love to come back one day and do a week or ten-day tramp over this famous track.

From here I retrace my route and drive south to Invercargill where I find a bunkhouse in a campground for twenty dollars. I am only a short distance from Bluff, the most southerly point of the South Island. I will save that for tomorrow, it is too late to start today. I pick up groceries for dinner and breakfast tomorrow, and go back to my cabin to relax for the evening.

Next morning I drive twenty-seven kilometers to Bluff and locate the huge signpost that has many arms pointing out in all directions showing distances to numerous cities including London, England at 18,958 kilometers. I enlist the help of a passer-by to take my picture under the post, then make my way to the trail leading up to the lookout.

A one hour tramp takes me uphill, winding through trees with very little else to see until reaching the top. The view from Bluff Point looks out over the Foueaux Strait to Stewart Island in the west and the South Pacific Ocean to the east. I am pleased with myself that I have the strength and endurance to do these tramps. I'm in better shape than I thought.

I tramp back down the trail and stop for lunch in Bluff before driving back to Invercargill. I find the visitor information centre and locate a youth hostel for tonight. It was newly opened about a year ago and looks very inviting. I check in and then do some browsing around the shops in town. Tomorrow is the end of January—where has the month gone?

The following morning is warm and sunny as I head around the southeast coast of the South Island. I make a stop at Curio Bay to see the Petrified Forest, Porpoise Bay (but do not see any dolphins), Matai to see the fabulous Horseshoe Falls, then on to Surat Bay Backpackers. It has been a long day, but with all the stops for pictures and short tramps I do not cover many kilometers. I especially want to stop at Surat Bay to see the Sea Lions basking on the beach.

I check into the backpacker home owned by Warren and Katherine. This is their private home that they have turned into a backpacker's residence with accommodations for about ten or twelve people. Warren and Katherine are between thirty-five and forty years old and love nature. I inquire about the sea lions and Warren gives me directions and a briefing for my safety on the beach.

Mid afternoon I don my runners and tramp out to the beach. I have to cross a small creek so I look for a shallow crossing, but even there the water is up to my knees. The trail takes me along a sandy bank then onto a very wide and long, sandy beach. I can see the sea lions in the distance and soon am within photo range. I am taking pictures as I walk and almost walk over one buried in the sand. *Okay Doris, pay closer attention.*

The only other people on the beach are two young backpackers from Surat Bay. I keep an eye on the sea lions as I continue down the beach making sure not to go between them and the water. This was the main piece of advice from Warren. "Don't block their escape route into the water," he said. One big old sea lion roars at me as I pass, possibly a little too close. All too soon I notice the tide coming in as the width of the beach becomes narrower, so start tramping back. I am careful to give them their space and am a bit nervous as the beach quickly disappears. I reach the creek without incident and cross once more, this time the water is up to my waist. Good thing the temperature is comfortable.

After dinner I drive out to Nugget Point and Roaring Bay to see the yellow-eyed penguins. Rain is coming down lightly and the wind is blowing hard as I tramp up the trail to the lighthouse at Nugget Point. I consider turning back but do not want to miss this great trail. Walking along the high ridge in this wind is a bit scary, but I make it and the view is well worth my effort.

From here I tramp down to Roaring Bay and the penguin lookout. Dusk has fallen now and I have to look hard to see the penguins. Soon I spot three on the beach and another one higher up on the rocks. Then another penguin magically appears, as if from thin air, on the beach. His exit from the water is instantaneous. Penguins swim all day for food then come out of the water at night. They mate for life and you can see them waddling around with their partner. They are so cute.

I make my way back up the trail in darkness to my car, and return to Surat Bay Backpackers. Another wonderful and fulfilling day!

Time is quickly slipping by—it is already the first of February. I try to squeeze as much into my day as possible. I can't bear the thought of missing anything, although I know I cannot possibly see it all in such a short time. My destination today is Dunedin, New Zealand's oldest city and first University City with loads of history and sights to see.

My drive to Dunedin takes me through a range of landscapes— green, sometimes rocky and grey—and is quite enjoyable in spite of the clouds and rain. South of Dunedin I leave Highway 1 and take the coastal road to Waihola. The road is a bit twisty and I notice a sign saying *SLOW DOWN*. A few meters farther another sign—*NO DOCTOR, NO HOSPITAL, ONE CEMETARY*. These people have a great sense of humor.

When I arrive in Dunedin I make my way to Octagon Square and seek out the visitor information centre. There is so much to see and do here that I organize my activities carefully to cover as much as possible. My first excursion is the road out to Otago Peninsula via Portobello Road. Portobello Road is very narrow, following the high cliff of the peninsula overlooking the Pacific Ocean on one side and the harbour on the other. Gorgeous views! On my way back from the point I drive up to the Royal Albatross Center situated high on the cliffs of Otago Peninsula. This is one of the very few places in the world where the Albatross can be found. These huge birds are white with black wings that span three meters. They can only fly where there is an adequate updraft to get them airborne. I am extremely fortunate for the winds this day. As I sit on the cliffs I can see two albatross gliding through the air—magnificent!

My last stop before leaving the peninsula takes me to the top of another hill to the Larnach Castle—another spectacular view overlooking the peninsula. Construction of the Larnach Castle began in 1871 and took five years to build and another eleven years to embellish the interior with the finest materials from around the world. William Larnach was an important political figure and former Minister of Mines. He shot himself in the head in Parliament House in 1898.

The Barker family bought the home, restored the gardens and castle, and opened it for tourist visits. The story told is that ghosts still occupy the castle. I wander through the gardens enjoying the serenity, aware that the castle is now closed and I should be leaving. I stop to talk to a lady tending the gardens. When I first speak to her she does not answer, but I persist and ask if that point I see to the north is the

Albatross Sanctuary. Only then does she look up and speak to me and I realize this is Margaret Barker I am talking to—the lady of the house. I am honoured and surprised that she would be working in her gardens. But then again, why not … why shouldn't she be out enjoying her incredible grounds?

I return to Dunedin, check into a hostel, have dinner and take one more drive. I head out to Seal Point Road and hike the sand dunes to another penguin viewing point. The hike going down the dunes is exhilarating; hiking back up is exhausting! I am certainly getting my exercise.

Next day is a relaxing 360-kilometer drive from Dunedin to Christchurch. I make several stops along the way to see more sights. At Moeraki I stop to view the huge, round boulders on the beach. These boulders are large rocks looking very much like volleyballs, formed from the sand rolling with the tide. Many of them must be over a meter in diameter. I arrive back in Christchurch around 5:00 PM and check into a backpackers lodge before phoning Bert Upjohn, my Servas contact. We make an appointment for 10:30 next morning and Bert gives me directions to their home. I spend a pleasant evening browsing around the shops in Christchurch Square and reflect on the fact that I am really here—living my dream.

At 10:30 next morning I arrive at the home of the Upjohn's. I meet Bert and Natalie and have a wonderful visit. Bert gives me an application form to fill out and asks me about my family, my work, my friends and my travels. His job is to interview and screen people wanting to join the Servas organization. We talk until noon and Natalie invites me to stay for lunch. I have enjoyed my visit with these folks, and for a nominal membership fee, am accepted as a member of Servas. Bert gives me the directory for New Zealand and explains how the organization works. It is up to the traveler to make contact with people in the directory. As a member one is allowed to stay two nights with a Servas host (unless invited to stay longer) and no money is to change hands. The organization is completely non-profit, the only cost being an annual membership fee to maintain the directories. It is acceptable to bring food, plan and make a meal, bring wine or a gift, and to help out whenever possible. This sounds just great and I cannot wait to make my first contact.

I try a couple of numbers before reaching Elizabeth Arlington.

Elizabeth and Helen are retired and live in South Shore at Pegasas Bay, just five kilometers from New Brighton and not far from Christchurch. They are delighted to have me stay with them. I find my way out to South Shore and meet my hosts. Helen is seventy years young and Liz is sixty-four. Helen takes me tramping along the beach and I find it difficult to keep up. Maybe I'm not in such good of shape after all!

I have a wonderful two days with these lovely ladies. I use my time wisely and book my passage on the Inter-Island Ferry that will take me to the North Island on February 14. Taking a vehicle is very expensive, so I decide not to take it. I will try to buy a car when I get to Wellington on the North Island. That means making arrangements to take a bus from Christchurch to Picton once I have returned this car.

All these arrangements made, I still have ten days to travel and see the east coast going north of Christchurch. I will monitor my time closely so as to get back to Christchurch in time to return the car and catch my bus to Picton.

On my drive up the east coast I am fortunate to stay with Servas hosts the entire way. The experiences I have could not have been found in a hostel, campground or hotel. Most of my hosts are retired and still very, very active. June and Rex, both in their seventies, hike, farm, show their flowers in competitions and do not look anywhere near their age. Rex tends to an acre of yard and gardens where he grows his prize plants and flowers. He has made paths leading down to a creek that empties into the Pacific Ocean. I try to remember all the flowers as I walk the paths through the trees. All kinds of roses, lilies, daisies, gladiolas, cannas, abundance trees with their coin-like leaves, blue spruce, yellow tipped cedar, fir, pine, palm, dogwood and much, much more than I recognize, line the paths and the yard. They have created their own little piece of heaven!

June is about my height, slight but sturdy built with gray hair, while Rex is tall and slim with gray hair. No hair dye necessary to make them look young. June takes me sight seeing and visiting friends at Gore Bay. These friends are in there eighties and look more like seventy. It must be something about this New Zealand air, or maybe their active lifestyles, that keep them young. Everyone I have met so far is an active tramper.

As we drive along the coast the wind is howling and the sea is raging, creating huge breakers. A storm is brewing along the coastlines of New Zealand and parts of Australia. Farther north, at Kaikoura, the surfing beaches are empty due to the high winds ravishing the coast.

June shows me a few other sights before returning to their farm in Cheviot. This is sheep sheering season and the sheep shearers are in the barn working right now. June gives me permission to go to the barn to witness the procedure. Two men are working on a 'stage-like' platform in the barn and a gal is in the pen with the sheep. They have a little assembly line going—the gal in the pen tosses up a sheep to the first man on deck, he hands the sheep over to the shearer who snares it between his legs and begins to sheer. In two or three minutes he is done and releases the bald sheep to another pen. I am amazed at how quickly the whole process is.

February 7, I continue north up the east coast to Blenheim. An angry, raging sea sends waves high into the air. As the waves crash against the rock banks, water sprays thirty meters into the air. Whale-watching tours have been put on hold until this weather system passes. I reach Blenheim quite early so continue on to Picton for lunch and check out the ferry I will be taking in a week. I take Queen Charlotte Drive winding around the mountains out to Queen Charlotte Sound. The drive is pleasant and once again I realize this would be a perfect ride with my motorcycle. I make my way back to Blenheim through grape-growing vineyards to the Blint's home, another Servas host. This is a family of pilots. Father, Collin, and two sons all fly. The oldest son's girlfriend is a fighter-jet pilot. Lorraine, the mother, is a teacher. I have a wonderful evening visiting with the Blint family and their young friends who have arrived for a weekend campout and to attend the Wine & Food Festival this weekend.

I spend the next day touring the winemaking area before continuing on to Nelson where I will meet Servas hosts Jill and Brian Kendrick. I cannot resist stopping to do a couple of short walks along the way. The Kendrick's home is built high on the side of a hill with an amazing view overlooking the Tasman Sea. Brian and Jill are about my age and both attend regular jobs, so they give me a key to the house and tell me to come and go as I please.

February 10, I am up early, have breakfast with my hosts, and am out the door at 9:00 AM to drive to Abel Tasman National Park— another very popular tramping track for hikers and backpackers. With Kahurangi National Park and Arthur Range to the west and the Tasman

Sea to the east, I start my tramp at Marahau and walk for two and a half hours following the trail through forests and overlooking bays, coves and beaches. I enjoy this trek so much I don't want to stop, but I still have to hike back to the car. The sun is shining and the wind is creating a warm, gentle breeze … it doesn't get much better than this.

For the past two weeks I have been communicating with Pauleen, a lady from Wellington, via the Internet. We made contact indirectly through reading Rita Golden Gelman's book *Tale of a Female Nomad*. Pauleen has offered to meet me at the ferry and give me a place to stay. The hospitality continues to be unbelievable!

Next morning I leave Nelson in the rain, but an hour and a half later the sun is shining. Sections of Highway 6 border the Kahurangi National Park where part of *Lord of the Rings* was filmed—probably much farther back into the park. Just knowing I am traveling in *their* part of the world is a special feeling. Highway 6 connects to Highway 7, which takes me across the Southern Alps, over the Lewis Pass, to the east coast and Christchurch.

I have made another Servas contact. I arrive at Diana's house in Christchurch about 5:30 PM, just before she is about to leave for the evening. Diana shows me around, gives me a key, and tells me to make myself at home. She apologizes for being too busy to entertain me, so I assure her that entertaining me is not necessary. Next morning I take the car back to A1 Rentals, and have to pay an extra $246 for a chip in the windshield that I just picked up two days ago. Peter very graciously covers the full $66 for the flat tire—I am happy about that. Peter's wife gives me a ride back to Christchurch Square where I catch a bus back to Diana's home. I am grateful to have time to myself so I can prepare my backpack for my trip to the North Island.

Chapter 5

New Zealand — North Island

February 14, Valentines Day, I have breakfast with Diana before catching my bus at 7:45 for Picton. The bus ride keeps its passengers swaying from side to side as it careens around one curve after another. The ride takes five hours and as time slips by I fear missing my ferry. We arrive in Picton at 12:45 PM with forty-five minutes to spare. I check in with my ticket and find out that the ferry is behind schedule due to recent high winds. The winds prevented the Lynx Ferry (fast ferry) from crossing earlier today and passengers are being transferred to this ferry, causing the delay.

Finally the ferry is loaded and departs, only half an hour late. I find a spot on the second floor at the bow of the ship next to the huge front windows. This ride turns out to be the roughest I have ever experienced! The ship lunges up and down bucking the waves, water splashing so hard and high it slaps soundly against the windows on the second deck. Passengers are getting sick all around me. I scan the room and notice people sitting in their seats and on the floor holding their head in one hand and a bag in the other. One trip to the bathroom makes me decide I can wait until I leave the ship. Every cubicle and sink is occupied with passengers getting sick. I am glad I took my seasickness capsule this morning.

Finally we dock. We arrive late and I am wondering if Pauleen will still be there or if she got tired of waiting. I have a written description of what she looks like and she has the same of me. I immediately start

73

scanning the crowd, asking anyone I think resembles my imaginary image, if she is Pauleen. Fifteen minutes later I still have not found her and resign myself to the fact that she has probably left. I am about to leave the terminal in search of a bus when a lady about my age and height with mid-length auburn hair comes towards me. "Are you Doris?" she asks. I am so glad to see her!

Pauleen's home is in Plimmerton, about a twenty-minute drive from Wellington. Her house is built on the side of a hill across the road from the Cook Strait. One would never tire of this fabulous view. I spend a few days with her and explore Wellington and area while she goes to work. On her day off, Pauleen takes me sightseeing going east and north of Plimmerton into the mountains.

I have decided to buy a cheap car instead of renting one here on the North Island. Pauleen suggests a local paper that lists a lot of used vehicles, and I set about phoning ads. After a few 'sorry it's sold' replies I find one that is still available. A young lady who is moving back to Australia is selling her little Suzuki. I do not want to miss this one so I immediately take the train, about three quarters of an hour, to Paraparaunu to meet Carlee. It still amazes me how easy it is to get around without a vehicle or my bike. Maybe I don't even need a car, but then I wouldn't have the freedom to stop whenever I choose.

Carlee's car is a little square four-door, standard stick shift, 1985 Suzuki. It appears to be in pretty good shape and the inside is clean. We go for a little test drive and I am thinking it runs pretty good. As long as it takes me around the North Island for the next three and a half weeks I will be happy. I offer her $500 and she takes it. I now have wheels. We transfer the registration, and inquire about insurance. I am given a few numbers for insurance agencies and call three of them, but no one will insure me. Finally I find an agent who is sympathetic and tells me that insurance is not mandatory and will be very expensive to buy. "I appreciate that you are trying to do the right thing," she says "but the New Zealand government makes it very difficult for foreigners to get insurance." I give it up and decide to drive without. I can hear the gasps as you read this. This will be the first of many times I am forced to drive/ride without insurance.

On February 20 I say goodbye to Pauleen and take highway 1 north to Taupo. Lake Taupo is New Zealand's largest lake and home of the famous *Ironman New Zealand*. I have made arrangements to meet

Servas hosts Chris and Larry Parton. The Partons are both teachers and offer a host of information about the area. They tell me there are many people training right now at Lake Taupo for the upcoming Ironman event to be held March 2.

A bit of trivia: February 20th, at 8:02 PM, the time and date reads: 20:02, 20/02, 2002.

Next day I cram in as much as I can. There is a lot of territory to cover and my time is passing quickly. On my agenda is Huka Falls, Craters of the Moon and Aratiatia Dam. I time my visit to the Dam so I can witness the gates being opened to allow water to rush down the canyon and create rapids. This is a daily occurrence at 10:00 AM, 12:00 noon, and 2:00 PM. Its purpose is to create extra power to service the busy times of day.

As I ride back into Taupo I notice hundreds of people lining the sides of the road leading into town and continuing right around the lake. There must be something going on, so I find a place to pull off the road, park and join the crowd. It does not take long to discover that Queen Elizabeth is on tour here. What a treat! I join the line of people and wait about an hour before her vehicle, complete with motorcycle escorts and an entourage of vehicles preceding, and following, pass slowly by the crowds. I have a great spot and can see her wave and smile at her audience.

February 22 to 26, I continue north through the steaming thermal fields of Rotorura and Kawerau, then to Ohope and follow Highway 35 around the peninsula that juts out on the east side of the North Island to Gisborne. Servas hosts are plentiful in New Zealand and I am able to stay at local homes all along the way. My hosts are wonderful! Bob and Jocelyn take me tramping on a trail to Tawerau Falls where the water emerges from a hole in the canyon wall. We climb the trail to the top of the falls then follow the river to where the water goes underground in two different places. In one spot the formation is like a basin. The water rushes in from smaller falls, swirls around the sides of the bowl and goes down a hole at the bottom—just like a bathroom sink or the flush of a toilet. It has been raining throughout our hour-and-a-half walk and we are soaked, but not cold. I would not have missed this for anything.

At Gisborne I stay with Wes and Barbara in their home on Poverty Bay. Poverty Bay is where Captain Cook made his first landing in New

Zealand on October 9, 1769. This is also where the big freighter got tossed into shallow waters during a storm in early February of this year (2002) and remained stuck on the sand for three weeks. Wes tells me that just this morning it got towed farther out to sea. He relates that for three weeks the ship was the major topic of discussion as they watched and waited for it to be towed away. The ship is still visible from their home along the beach.

I do an historical walk of Gisborne that includes the Margaret Sievwright memorial in the Rose Gardens. Margaret Sievwright lived from 1844 to 1905 and was prominent in the suffragist movement when women won the right to vote in 1893. On her memorial is this quote: *"What do women want? We want men to stand out of our sunshine, that is all."* Margaret Sievwright

There is much to see and photograph in Gisborne. I locate the Totem Pole that was donated by the Government of Canada in 1969 for the bicentennial of Captain Cook's landing at Poverty Bay. I do not recall this event, but at that time in my life I was not thinking outside my little corner of the world.

February 26, I head northwest on Highway 2 across the Raukumara Mountain Range towards Opotiki. Don't you just love these names? New Zealand is home of the Maori nation, hence the names come from the Maori language. I have come from Poverty Bay at Gisborne to the Bay of Plenty at Opotiki. These Bays were named by Captain Cook on his voyages to chart New Zealand. On the east coast, in the little harbour at Gisborne, his crew ran into problems with Maori tribes and was not able to take on supplies, thus the name *Poverty Bay* was born. In the *Bay of Plenty*, a much larger bay on the north side of the cape, the crew was met with friendly welcomes and provisions were plentiful. Sandy beaches stretch all along the bay, fruit is plentiful and the climate is mild. The area is known for its kiwi orchards. I stop along the Bay of Plenty for a good look at White

Island through my binoculars. I can see the steam rising from the volcano, which gives White Island its name. My final destination for today is Mount Maunganui where I will stay with Servas hosts Dave and Shirley Gill.

Dave and Shirley live in an adult community development and are very active people. Dave will take me hiking up Mount Maunganui trail in the morning. Shirley apologizes that she cannot come because her muscles are sore from the aerobics class she started yesterday. Shirley is only seventy years young. Oh, how I admire these people.

In the morning Dave and I leave after breakfast to do our hike. Shirley warns me not to be upset if I can't keep up. "*I* can't even keep up to Dave most days," she says. Dave is seventy-nine!

The base of the trail is quite gentle and I do just fine keeping pace with Dave and his long legs, but soon we start the climb up the most difficult part of Mount Maunganui to the peak. The trail is steep and reaches up almost three hundred meters. I am huffing and puffing and have to stop several times to catch my breath. Not Dave—he has not even broken into a sweat. Finally I reach the top and soak in the view of the Bay of Plenty and surrounding area. "I have to rest a few minutes," I say to Dave. He is ready to turn around and start right back down. I guess he has done the trail and seen the view enough times that he just goes for the exercise. I am totally in awe of the fitness level of the retired people I have met in New Zealand. This would be a great place to retire.

I continue north along the coast making many stops to hike, take pictures, and sightsee along the way. I am told about Clark Island—a little island off Whiritoa Beach that is accessible by foot at low tide. I throw my shoes in the boot of the car, roll up my pant legs and cross to the island. The water is warm, like a cool bath, and never over my knees. I reach the Island in fifteen minutes, explore a few coves and take pictures before starting back. I don't linger too long as I do not want to be caught when the tide starts to roll in.

As I drive these twisty roads and enjoy the scenery I see a sign saying *Home of Topadahill*. Well now, that is just curious enough that I need to see for myself. I follow a winding road up the hills overlooking the ocean until I reach the top of the hill. Sure enough there is an art studio called *Home of Topadahill*. The property sits at one of the highest spots, overlooking the ocean and Whaiekawa Harbour, and is surrounded by lush green rolling hills and valleys. The world-renowned, French artist *Guity* owns this charming piece of paradise. The stunning views from here would be an inspiration to any artist. I stop for a short visit and admire her little gallery of artwork.

Continuing on, I stop for a couple of hours at Hot Water Beach, so named because of the hot pools that bubble up through the sand from underground. Then I hike out to Cathedral Cove at Hahei and drive the gravel road that winds along a high cliff ledge to Opito Bay. Here I stay with Servas hosts Eric and Brenda. Their home is located on the tip of the Coromandel Peninsula and quite isolated. The weather has turned cloudy and rainy and I hope it does not rain too much and make a mess of the road I just traveled on to get here—there is not other exit. I use this dreary weather time to catch up on my e-mails, newsletters, and update my Web site.

I spend a couple of days traveling around the beautiful Coromandel Peninsula and take the famous Highway 309 to visit some well known tourist spots. On my way back I have an accident. I am driving carefully, as the gravel road is narrow and twists its way around the hills with the cliff on one side and the bank on the other. I am not driving fast, but the tires get caught in loose gravel. The car fishtails, spins around on the road and hits the bank. As my little car is spinning out of control I am intensely aware of the steep cliff on one side. I try to maneuver towards the bank and am stopped abruptly, crashing with the left front fender into the bank. I am shaken up a bit but am able to get out. As I climb out of the car three European tourists walk over to see if I am okay. They had been traveling behind me and witnessed the whole thing.

We examine the car—the front left fender is crunched and the headlight and signal light are broken. As far as we can tell that is the extent of the damage. These wonderful people help me push the car out of the shallow ditch and back onto the road, make sure it runs, then continue on their way. I am ever so grateful for their help.

A stop at a panelbeater shop (auto body shops in NZ are called panelbeaters) produces an estimate of $371 to repair the damages. I don't think I will be doing that since I only paid $500 for the car. I decide to continue on my journey and try again once I reach Auckland.

After a few phone calls in Auckland I discover that getting my car repaired will be very expensive. I decide to pull out my *Gold Book* and call GWRRA member, Bryan Ham. Would you believe it? He just happens to be a panelbeater! Bryan tells me where to pick up the lights and to bring my car out to his place—he will see what he can do. Next morning I pick up the parts and drive out to Papakoura to meet Bryan and his wife Phil. About four hours later, while I visit with Phil, Bryan has the fender straightened, the lights back in and my car looking good as ever. A mechanic friend stops by the garage, cleans the air filter and adjusts the carburetor. I am ready to roll again. Bryan refuses to accept payment and says "I'm just glad I could get you back on the road." Goldwing riders are really great people.

The date is March 8 when I leave Auckland. I have one week to reach the farthest north point of the North Island and return to Auckland, sell my car, and catch my plane back to Melbourne, Australia.

I head north on Highway 1 along the east coast of this very narrow strip of the Island, stopping at Orewa, Manawhai Cliffs, and Paihia, which borders the Bay of Islands. I book into a Backpacker lodge and go walking up the beach. Next day I drive to Matauri Bay and Kerikeri and find New Zealand's oldest stone building, built in 1835; and oldest wood building, built in 1822. They are situated in a lovely setting along the Kerikeri River. Matauri Bay is a wonderful spot to catch a glimpse of the islands scattered throughout the Bay.

March 10 I continue north on Highway 10 to Kaitaia, passing by several bays and harbors. I check into the Mainstreet Backpackers then make arrangements for the bus trip on ninety-mile beach to Cape Regina. Taking a vehicle is too risky and I am advised to take the bus tour. I'm happy with that but cannot leave without saying I have driven on ninety-mile beach. After a few inquiries I am told I can access the most southwesterly end of the beach at Ahipara. So off I go in my little car and drive out onto the sand. The sand is quite well packed and my car is light, so I have no problem getting close to the water to take a couple of pictures. It has been a good day. I drive back to Kaitaia and prepare for tomorrows bus trip.

Early next morning I catch the Harrisons Cape Road Runner bus for the tour to Cape Regina—almost the farthest point north on the Island. Our driver is Kinge, a Maori native who knows this land well. He shares a wealth of information and entertains us with Maori folk songs as we travel along to the Cape. When he reaches the north point of Cape Regina he stops the bus and we all walk out to the lighthouse, battling the winds along the way. Standing at the end of this narrow peninsula overlooking the Tasman Sea and the Pacific Ocean you can actually distinguish where these two great bodies of water meet by their different shades of blue. From here we stop at a small beach on Tapotupotu Bay and have our lunch. Shortly after continuing, Kinge drives into the water of Te Paki Stream on hard packed sand, eventually arriving at the Sand Dunes. We make a stop here and everyone gets a turn or two at tobogganing down the dunes. The climb up the steep, hard packed sand is difficult, but well worth the thrill of sliding down. The child within comes out to play.

The tour of ninety-mile beach is very dependent on the tide. If the tide is too high the bus ride back is just a repeat of the trip up. Right now the tide is low and Kinge keeps his bus on the hard packed sand between the waters edge and the soft dry sand. He relays to us that this stretch is called ninety-mile beach, but in fact, is only ninety kilometers. He points out a dead car buried in the sand and stops for us to get out, have a look and take pictures. "This is a tourist vehicle that didn't make it and was left to die in the sand," he says with a grin. Another stop allows us to walk on the beach and get our feet wet in the Tasman Sea. After leaving the beach Kinge makes a stop at the Kauri Kingdom where ancient kauri trees, dug from a number of buried prehistoric forests, are handcrafted into furniture, art, crafts and gifts. These trees are known to be the oldest workable timbers in the world.

Our route back to Kaitaia takes us through the Aupouri Forest—the largest man made forest in the Southern Hemisphere. Pines are planted here especially for harvesting.

It is still early afternoon when I arrive back in Kaitaia, so I load my things into the car and drive to Opononi/Omapere, twin towns bordering each other, on the Hokianga Harbour. What a gorgeous place—unspoiled by large numbers of tourists, boasting lovely beaches, good swimming, and a beautiful harbour and is only fifteen minutes from the Kauri forest and forty minutes from the nearest shopping.

I find a room for sixteen dollars at a Backpackers residence on the hill overlooking the harbour. This is my last overnight stop before reaching Auckland and returning to Australia. I relax on the large deck facing the harbour and do some writing. There is a sign on the office door advertising "For sale, lease, or new manager wanted". If I were not just beginning my journey around the world, I would check this out.

Next morning I go down to the information centre, browse through their museum and watch the video of Opo, the dolphin who became famous to Omapere Beach. This is a very peaceful place with fantastic beaches and stunning views. It would be a lovely place to live.

I continue my drive south along the coast to Auckland stopping in the kauri forest to see the giant kauri tree. "Tane Mahuta" is Maori for "Lord of the Forest" and the largest living kauri tree in New Zealand. It's girth is 13.7 meters (45 ft.) which is 4.4 meters (14 ft.) in diameter, trunk height before the branches start is 17.7 meters (58 ft.), total height 52 meters (169 ft.), and is estimated to contain 245 cubic meters (8,630 cu. ft) of timber. I look and feel like an ant beside this huge giant!

Some of the roads I take along the west coast follow the top rims of old craters providing fabulous views of green valleys on either side with rolling hills, trees and rivers. I arrive in Auckland and call on Betty, the Servas host I stayed with here a week ago. She welcomes me once again and I appreciate her hospitality. This will be my last two nights in New Zealand.

I take a drive to One Tree Hill overlooking Auckland with views of the harbour, and then make my way downtown before going back to Betty's. One of Betty's boarders, Mark, age fifty-eight, wants to buy my car. Mark is a Chinese exchange student and has never driven here in New Zealand, so I take him out for a drive. He decides that he wants the car so we stop at the government office to fill out the transfer papers. He pays me five hundred dollars and we are both happy.

March 15, 2002, I catch a taxi to the airport and fly from Auckland back to Melbourne. I love it here in New Zealand, you can bet I will be back.

Chapter 6

Australia, Part II

March 15, I arrive back in Australia and meet with a Servas host before returning to Curtis and Vanessa's flat. I am happy to see them both again. My stay this time will be brief, as I will start my travels shortly.

I pick up my bike the next day, ride into the city and park on the sidewalk in line with the dozens of other bikes. I smile as I think of my biking friends back home. I must send them a picture, because parking on the sidewalk there would warrant a ticket. I do some shopping at Peter Stevens Motorcycle shop and when I return I find two fellows seriously looking over my bike. I hurry to the bike and say, "Hi, can I help you?" Turns out these two fellows, Eric and Jason, are Magna riders and invite me on a ride around Tasmania with their Magna Club. I also discover they are both computer techs and they offer to help solve the problem I've been having connecting my laptop to the Internet. Eric and Jason are about 30, Eric has a head of black hair and Jason is bald. Eric is only about 5'7", while Jason is two or three inches taller. They both ride Honda Magnas and sound like they have a lot of fun with their friends and bikes.

Wow, this is great! I wasn't planning on going to Tasmania but now I cannot pass up this opportunity. Later I meet Nene, Eric's girlfriend, who rides her own Magna. Nene gives me the details of the Tasmania ride. The group will be leaving on Saturday, March 23, and Nene is quite sure that they secured the last spots available on the ferry. I will have to make my own arrangements to cross the ocean. Not a problem, I will check the schedules and meet them on the other side. I am able to get a booking on the Spirit of Tasmania for Thursday, March 21.

I have a few days to fill so I accept an invitation from Servas host, Merle Sloan, to attend a social function with the Victoria Servas group. On Sunday I ride out to Western Port, a lovely treed area bordering the water, and have the pleasure of meeting several Servas members. Over a casual buffet meal I listen to their stories about their experiences traveling and staying with Servas members around the world. This is wonderful! Along with my great experiences in New Zealand, I can rest assured Servas is a very reputable group of people worldwide.

Next day I take my computer into the city to Eric, who works for Telstra. He works on it for several hours but cannot make an Internet connection. Eric is not a quitter. He tells me he does not like to be defeated, especially when he knows we should be able to connect. I leave my computer with him for the day so he can work on it in the evening. I sure hope he can figure it out.

March 19, I stop in at Telstra to see Eric. He has been successful. I am so grateful, now I can upload my Web site. I pay a visit to Nene, who also works for Telstra, and get the update on our Tasmania trip. She informs me there are twelve people coming in their group, a few of them riding two-up. We will travel a route that Eric and Nene have mapped out, taking us around the island of Tasmania. I will be crossing on the 21st to Devonport and their group will be crossing on the 23rd to George Town, where I will meet up with them. I am looking forward to the ride and their company.

March 21, I cross the Bass Strait on the Spirit of Tasmania and arrive in Devonport at 9:00 AM. I check into the Tasman House Backpackers before going for a ride. I head south to do a loop around the Great Lake, which is surrounded by The Great Western Tiers—mountains as high as 1,392 meters. The road twists, rises and dips, becoming cold in the high mountain passes and remaining warm in the valleys. On my way around the east side of Great Lake I spot a wombat about twenty meters off the side of the road. I stop and pull out my camera. I cannot believe how big he is! I certainly would not want to run into him on the road. After a wonderful ride, and all too soon, I am back in Devonport.

Back at the Tasman House I check my Servas directory and make a couple of calls. I contact Jenny at Launceston and Brian and Faye at Hobart. Jenny invites me to stay with her tomorrow night and I graciously accept.

I spend the next day traveling to Launceston. The scenery is unbelievable here and I stop many times for pictures. Launceston is on the south end of River Tamar with the road following close along the west side of the river crossing occasionally to the east. At the most southern tip of River Tamar I stop for a long walk on Cataract Gorge Trail. The trail follows completely around the Gorge on the edge of the cliffs crossing the river on a swinging suspension bridge. What a fabulous day! At 5:00 PM it is time to find Jenny's home. I have arranged to meet her for dinner and a movie.

Next morning I spend a leisurely time visiting with Jenny before riding to George Town to meet the other riders from Melbourne. They crossed the Bass Strait on the Cat Ferry today. After a few introductions we begin our ride to St. Helens on the east coast bordering Georges Bay. My friends have made a previous booking in a lodge and I am able to share with some of them—just one of the many benefits of traveling with a group.

Leaving St. Helens next morning Ian makes some great emergency maneuvers to avoid hitting a dog that runs out in front of him. He skids down the pavement a few meters eventually coming to a stop in the middle of the road. He comes out with a few scratches to his shiny red Magna and some bruised muscles to himself. The dog disappears without a backward glance. Ian relates to us later that his thoughts, as he was skidding down the pavement, were … "not to scratch my new helmet." We all had a good laugh about that. We take some time to relax and calm down while the guys straighten out some bent metal. Back on the road about an hour later we continue on the Tasman highway to Sorell, then the Arthur highway to Port Arthur on a narrow peninsula on the south east coast.

We stop at Port Arthur for the night. I am unable to get accommodations with the group so I check into a clean and comfortable hostel up on a hill overlooking Port Arthur Historical site and Carnarvon Bay. This is the historic site of Port Arthur penal settlement built in 1832. At that time Tasmania was called Van Diemen's Land and was the most feared destination for British convicts. In 1856 the first parliament was elected and Van Diemen's Land was changed to Tasmania in an effort to escape its dreadful penal reputation.

Very early next morning I walk down to the gates of the historical site. The ticket booth is closed. I don't want to miss going through this old penitentiary site so I walk around until I find a way down some cliffs. I am very careful to stay out of sight while I do a self-guided tour of the old buildings, the remaining cells and the grounds. Just as I am finishing the last section I hear voices. As I carefully sneak around the corner I see Nene and Aaron doing the same thing. We chuckle about sneaking into the sight and quickly find our way out before the gate attendants arrive for their morning shift.

After breakfast we begin our ride to New Norfolk where the group made reservations at a motel. The morning starts out cloudy but luck is with us and the sky clears up to provide a sunny day. We do a leisurely ride so we can enjoy the great twisty roads and breathtaking scenery, making stops at several interesting historical towns along the way. I have made arrangements to stay with Servas hosts Brian and Faye in Hobart, so I split from the group late afternoon and will meet up with them tomorrow morning to ride to Southport.

Hobart is a lovely old city bordering both sides of the River Derwent. Hobart and Launceston are homes to the University of Tasmania.

I don't have any trouble finding Brian and Faye's address. Brian meets me with a big smile as I pull into his driveway. He used to own a motorcycle so he is excited to see my bike and find out about my journey. He makes sure my bike is parked safely in his garage before we go in for dinner. I have a wonderful evening visiting with my new friends.

March 26, I meet up with the gang for our ride out to Southport, located at the south point of Tasmania. What a gorgeous ride through hills and valleys, often paralleling a river. We stop at several ports and bays along the way. I decide to leave the group and get off the main road for awhile, only to end up in eight kilometers of gravel road that has been freshly watered down. This road is not fun for any kind of bike but I make it through okay. One mishap today—Aaron slid out on loose gravel in a corner and went down. No serious injury or bike damage. I would say we have angels watching over our little group.

After a second night in Hobart and New Norfolk we are off to Mt. Field National Park. We hike into Russell Falls then regroup for our ride to Strathgordon, in the Franklin-Gordon National Park.

Oops, another little accident—Maria does not quite make a curve and ends up in the ditch on the other side. Those who saw the incident said she rode like a pro, staying on right to the end. Again, no serious injury to rider or bike. We are definitely being looked after.

Strathgordon is located on the edge of the vast Southwest National Park and surrounded by rugged mountain ranges. The village was originally built in 1969 as a construction village for workers on the Gordon Dam. The dam flooded Lake Pedder and Lake Gordon covering over five hundred square kilometers to hold twenty-seven times the volume of water in Sydney Harbour. There is not much of a village left now, just a motel and visitor center for the few tourists and trampers who make it out this far. The sky has clouded over and rain drizzles steadily. Hopefully it will end before morning.

At dinner tonight Colleen said; "I couldn't finish my tea." I'm thinking *that's odd*. Sometime later I realize that *tea* means *dinner*. Back in Hobart at Brian and Faye's, Faye asked me if I had had tea. I replied with "No, I had lasagna and a beer." She must have thought I was a bit daft.

In the morning the rain has stopped but the air is very cool. I start out with my heated jacket plugged in. We decide to ride in smaller groups now because of the wide range of riding experience. My rear tire is looking pretty awful so I slow it down considerably and ride alone so as not to impede anyone else. I make several stops for pictures and check the tire each time.

Farther up the west coast, on the way to Strahan, I pass through Queenstown and miles of open cut copper mining. The Lyell highway twists its way up Mt. Lyell with tight hairpin turns and steep edges overlooking the mining pits. Once at the top I make my way down the long, twisty road into Queenstown, then on to Strahan.

Strahan is a popular town for tourists and offers a cruise up the Macquarie Harbour. Most of our group joins the cruise. The captain does a short stop on Sarah Island, which once housed a penal settlement for re-offenders. The tour guide and commentator do a fabulous job and keep us entertained and in suspense. The weather at Strahan is rainy and cloudy with the occasional patch of sun.

From Strahan we ride to Zeehan and on the Murchison highway before turning off to Cradle Mountain National Park. We book into cabins at Cradle Mountain Lodge, nestled at the foot of Cradle Mountain. The accommodations include a huge buffet breakfast next morning. Some of us do the two-hour hike around Dove Lake. Very pretty! After dinner that evening several possums and a potaroo pay us a visit. One of the possums wanders into a cabin and makes himself comfortable on Jason's pillow.

Early next morning I go for a walk. The temperatures dropped overnight and the roof tops are covered with ice. Our bikes have frost on the windshields and seats. The sun is shining and the air is crisp and it feels very much like home after the first frost. What a peaceful setting—I am the only person out here this early in the morning. I get some incredible reflection pictures over the little pond with the ice crystals glistening in the trees. Cradle Mountain Lodge is a lovely place and, although fully booked, the grounds spread out enough that it never seems packed with people.

March 31, it is time to head home. I mean back to Melbourne, of course. I ride with Aaron as far as Sheffield where I say my goodbyes to the group and continue on to Devonport. The group heads to George Town where they catch the ferry back to Melbourne. My back tire is showing a wide strip of cord around half the tire! Needless to say, I am traveling quite slowly. I just need to get back to the ferry—my bike is booked in for tires and a service job as soon as I return to Melbourne.

I arrive back in Devonport safely and still have several hours before my ferry leaves. Jenny, my host from Launceston, has invited me to have Easter dinner with her family. She has to come right through Devonport so she stops to pick me up and I am treated to a wonderful Easter meal with her Mom, Dad, three sisters and her son and daughter. Easter dinner in Tasmania with more newfound friends—I feel very blessed.

Tasmania is a wonderful island to tour on a motorcycle. It is Australia's only island state and most of its wilderness area remains virtually unspoiled. The national parks contain some of the best tramping tracks in the world and the scenery throughout the entire island is gorgeous. Roads are smooth with very little traffic, and for all you motorcycling enthusiasts there is no end to curves and hills.

I arrive back in Melbourne at 3:00 PM on April 1. The rear tire on my bike is *really bald!* I call Nene and Eric to thank them for inviting me on this trip. I am very grateful to have had this opportunity to meet these wonderful people and ride with them.

Next morning I ride my bike to Peter Steven's motorcycle shop for a service job and tires. The service technician is shocked at the state of my tire and wonders how I managed to get that far on it. All I can say is that my angels were looking after me.

The mechanics do a full service on the bike including replacing the chain. The sprockets are good so there is no need to change them. It feels good to have the bike back in top-notch shape and riding on a full set of rubber.

April 7, I say my goodbyes to Curtis and Vanessa once again and leave to start my journey up the east coast of Australia to Cairns, then west to Darwin where I will fly to Singapore. There is a lot to see and do along this coast and I know there won't be time to experience it all. The sun is shining and I am excited to continue my journey.

My first stop is Wilson's Promontory. There are many great beaches and tramping trails in the park, as there are throughout all of Australia. I choose Mount Oberon and hike to the summit at 558 meters above sea level. A one-hour steady climb gets me to the top where I enjoy a spectacular 360-degree view. What a great feeling sitting at the top of the summit and looking out over the ocean, trees and beaches. I relax and enjoy the view for a few minutes before hiking back to the parking lot and my bike. I am pleased that no one has touched anything on my bike. I had left my riding clothes, boots and helmet thrown across the top of the handlebars and returned to find them just as I left them.

I have to make a stop at Squeaky Beach just to see if it really squeaks. The sand is white and very fine—so fine that it squeaks underfoot as you walk across it. Yes, it squeaks! Now that I have my boots off I figure I might as well enjoy the sand and water.

Over the next couple of days I ride through many interesting places stopping to take pictures and enjoy the sights. Eagle Point provides a lovely view of the silt jetties. On April 9 I reach Lakes Entrance and stop at servas hosts Eric and Jenny Patton. Eric is tall (over six feet) and Jenny about five-foot four. They are high-energy people and love having servas guests. Jenny is excited to show me around. She is such a wonderful lady. She takes me sightseeing and introduces me to some fascinating people—Maria is a pilot and sailor of her own yacht; Lynn is an artist and has King Parrots and Crimson Roselles that feed in her bird feeders; John is a vet who collects and restores motorcycles and old cars. John shows me his collection of bikes and cars. He has about seven motorbikes—amongst them are a 1917 Emblem and 1923

AJS. I have never heard of them before. He also has an old Douglas, Triumph, BMW, Honda and one other that I cannot recall. What a wonderful day. I would never have met these people if it were not for servas hosts like Jenny.

On our way back home we make a stop at the fishing boats on the dock where I buy a bucket of fresh prawns. What a treat this is! Jenny makes fish and prawns for dinner. There is nothing like a fresh catch.

I do a day ride to Dinner Plain and Mt. Hotham on the Great Alpine Road. I cross the Great Dividing Range into Alpine National Park in Australia's Southern Alps. There is a ski hill up here—not open at the moment, as their winter has not yet begun. I am on a road that follows the top of a mountain ridge and when I look to my left I can see the top of four other mountain ridges off in the distance. It has been a wonderful day for a ride, the roads are great and the sun has been shining all day. I head back to the Patton's home for one more night before continuing on to Canberra.

I leave Lakes Entrance on April 14 and head north towards Canberra, the Australian Capital Territory. Today I will leave Victoria and cross into New South Wales. The sky is covered in clouds and sometime throughout the day it begins to rain. By the time I reach Canberra and the home of Servas hosts Pat and Bill, I am soaked.

Canberra is a well-planned city with the government buildings in the centre and everything going out from there. One does not get the feeling of driving in a city at all. The main arteries take you out to ring roads that surround the city and to the residential areas which are hidden from the highways behind tree belts. Some people detest the layout but I find it easy to navigate. There are all kinds of things to do here—from hiking or cycling the trails through the parks and around a scenic man-made lake, to visiting a number of interesting museums and art galleries. Pat takes me sight seeing and up to the top of Black Mountain Lookout. We go to the top of the Telstra Tower to obtain the greatest view. From here we get a 360-degree view of Canberra—Wow! Over the next two days Pat and I cycle twenty-two kilometers around the man-made lake in the city (just a bit more strenuous than riding my motorcycle) then go horseback riding on the outskirts of Canberra. It has been a long time since I have ridden a horse, but I do just fine. Kangaroos are bounding around out in the paddock and on our return the sun is setting and the white cockatoos are screeching their heads off. What a treat to add to my many adventures.

About four months ago, when I camped in Port Augusta I met a man named Matti Svahn, his brother visiting from Finland, and their friend Tony. Matti is from Finland and married Jenny, an Australian lady, some thirty years ago and settled in Canberra. He invited me to call on him and his wife when I arrive. April 16 I give them a call and Matti invites me to stay with them a few days. I will go there tomorrow afternoon.

I arrive at the Svahn's home around 4:00 PM and am met by Matti's wife, Jenny; and his niece and sister who are visiting from Finland. Shortly after my arrival Tony stops in for a visit. Jenny introduces me by saying, "This is Tony, he's a widower." I can't help but wonder if they are trying to do some match making. I push the thought aside and just enjoy the company of these wonderful people. Matti and Jenny are near retirement age and are avid golfers. Matti is an engineer, tall and very slim, with graying hair. Jenny is about five-foot five, a little on the heavy side, with reddish hair. They have no children but love to have people visit. Jenny is a fabulous cook and we enjoy a great dinner much like a good old country dinner my mother would have made.

I spend three nights with the Svahns. One day I ride to Gibralter Falls, the old Satelite Tracking Station at Cranberry Creek, and the new Tracking Station not far away. I had no idea Australia played such a big role in America's space projects. I tour the government buildings; Old Parliament House and New Parliament House (which is built underground); the Aboriginal Embassy (a three sided shell with a slanted roof, all made of plywood and painted in vibrant colors); and some art galleries in the city. On Saturday morning I pack my bike to leave amidst great protests from Matti. He insists I should stay longer. Before I leave he calls his family in Finland and arranges for me to stay with them if I make it to their country. Then he says "I would have arranged a balloon ride for you if you'd have stayed longer." I am almost tempted to unpack my bike and stay. I am sad to leave these wonderful people but I have a lot of country to cover yet, so off I go towards Sydney.

After riding in heavy fog for about an hour, the air clears and the sun begins to shine. The highway to Sydney is wide and smooth and for a long distance I battle strong crosswinds. I do not spend a lot of time in Sydney—just long enough to find Darling Harbour, the Sydney Harbour Bridge and the Opera House. The Opera House is an amazing work of architecture, very unique with its sail like roof structures. I ride to Bondi Beach where the Olympic volleyball championships were held a summer or two ago. The beach curves in a crescent shape around the edge of Bondi Bay and is very inviting.

I continue to ride in rain and fog most of the day as I head north on the coastal highway. Over the next eight days my stops take me to Newcastle, Forster, Lismore, the Gold Coast and Byron Bay (the most easterly point on the mainland of Australia), before leaving New South Wales and entering Queensland. I stay with Servas hosts and at youth hostels along the coast. All of these places are interesting with fantastic scenery, great weather and terrific people. One Servas host has over twenty different varieties of fruit trees growing in her yard—would I love to live there!

May 1, I leave New South Wales and cross into Queensland. My first stop is Palm Beach, on the Gold Coast. I stay with Jen, a contact I made through a friend of a friend of a friend. I am really beginning to feel that it's a small, small world. It seems that somehow our spirits are connected to people and places far unknown to us.

The Gold Coast is another popular tourist area with numerous high-rise buildings, great sandy beaches, fabulous weather, and is known as Surfers Paradise. I do not linger here, but instead take a ride up Tamborine Mountain. Riding the winding road to the top of the mountain ridge, enjoying the incredible scenery along the way, and breathing in the fresh air, puts me in biker's paradise. On my way back I somehow get on the wrong road and end up right back at Surfers Paradise. Oh well, no harm done, I will just continue on from here.

My next stop is Redland Bay to have lunch with a Servas host and avid biker. I arrive at Ron Grants home about noon and am invited in for lunch. I soon find out that Ron is a transplant from Canada. He has lived in Australia for over thirty years and has a sister and mother living in Edmonton, Alberta. I enjoy my short visit with this entertaining and eccentric fellow before continuing on to Brisbane, the Capital of Queensland, and the Sunshine Coast.

At Noosa Heads, near the north end of the Sunshine coast, I locate Servas hosts Tony and Helen. My stay with these wonderful people is like staying in a five star hotel. I am given a beautifully decorated room with my own private bathroom. The first morning we walk to the beach and go swimming in the ocean before coming home to a wonderful breakfast created by both Helen and Tony. That afternoon they take me sight seeing. The second morning Helen and I do an eight-kilometer walk while Tony goes running, then we go for coffee with the ladies running club. This is the life! I really can't think of a better way to start my day. Maybe this is where I will retire some day.

I have been having so much fun sight seeing and meeting new friends that I have not been putting on too many kilometers each day. On Saturday, May 4, I decide to cover more ground and actually ride 540 kilometers. That is still not a hard day of riding and I am able to make several stops along the coast before turning west to Mount Morgan—on another road made for biking.

I arrive at Servas hosts Cathy and Ian's home about 5:00 PM. They live out in the country and my instructions from Cathy are to follow the windy road off the highway and watch for the signs that say *Struck Oil*. I am really out in the country. Farms along the road are quite a distance apart. I leave the pavement and follow a dirt road for about four kilometers, crossing Texas gates and a couple of mud holes before finally reaching the end of the road and the home of Ian and Cathy. They show me around very briefly before showing me to my house. I have a three-bedroom cottage all to myself, down the hill about two hundred meters from the big house.

Cathy and Ian invite me up to the big house for dinner at 7:00 PM, so I unpack my bike and have time to clean up and settle in. About 6:45 I walk up the hill for dinner. The night is very dark and I have to use the torch (flashlight) Cathy lent me to find my way. I am a little edgy and aim my light into the dark shadows as I walk at a hurried pace, my heart racing.

Over dinner Cathy and Ian fill me in on their property, which is a conservation area. "We have made a few hiking trails through the bush which you can explore tomorrow. We have set traps in the bush for the wild pigs and go out to check them each morning. You can come with us if you like," says Ian. "Oil was never found in this area but there was gold, silver and copper mined at Mount Morgan, the town you came through earlier."

Cathy adds, "There are no locks on the doors of the house you're in but we are far out in the country and quite safe. Don't pay any mind to the possums—at night they like to get into the roof gables and make a bit of noise."

Oh dear, I'm going to be so scared I won't be able to sleep at all.

After a simple, but excellent, dinner I start walking back to my house. Still very dark out and I am feeling a bit nervous, until I look up and see the sky full of stars. They seem to be just over the treetops—I feel like I could reach up and touch them. I have never witnessed stars so close. I keep my torch moving into the shadows as I walk, and spot a wallaby at the edge of the trees. Back at the house I stay out on the deck for awhile to watch the stars. I experience such a feeling of peacefulness that I am able to push all my earlier fears aside.

Next morning I am up at 6:00 o'clock to go with Ian and Cathy to check the wild pig traps. We head out onto their property in an old 4-wheel drive farm truck, making our way through the hills and trees. A couple of hills are so steep I wonder if the truck will make it up, but Ian knows exactly what he is doing—shift her down to low and bump and bounce to the top. Their job today, after checking the pig traps, is to dig lantana (a noxious tree that spreads and chokes out the good trees) until noon. When we arrive at the far end of the property Ian gives me a map of some walking trails and tells me to take a hike (well … not exactly like that). I am a bit nervous about hiking out here alone, afraid I will get lost. Cathy tells me to just stay put if I get lost and they will look for me if I am not back at the house when they return. With that reassurance I start tramping.

This track is not the well-trodden and groomed tracks I have been accustomed to these past few months, but a much less used track through the bush. The map Ian gives me is hand drawn but looks easy enough to follow. I tramp over and around rock boulders, zig-zagging back and forth across a little creek and up to high lookout points. At one turn, on Rocky Gully Track, I have to get around a huge boulder. *Not much room on the ledge,* I am thinking as I carefully make my way around. Then I come to Rock Creek and cannot see where the trail leads from here. I climb out to the face of the rocks and take a look around. The track is behind me, the same way I came except one level lower on the hill. I have to follow the creek a few meters then drop down on the track below. I continue, stopping at any lookout points I come to. Along the trail I see a rainbow parrot with brilliant colors of green, yellow, blue and red. About two hours later I am back at the cottage feeling very proud of my accomplishment. This was quite a different hike and I am glad I accepted the challenge.

I spend the afternoon drawing in my sketchbook and relaxing on the balcony watching the birds play in the birdbath and chase each other from tree to tree. Two different species of birds share the bath and three different species line the branches of the trees. Nature is so wonderful.

Two easy day rides gets me to Townsville where I take a forty-minute ferry ride to Magnetic Island. I spend two nights on the Island in a luxurious bed and breakfast home with servas hosts Terri and Graham. I can tell I am getting very spoiled by all this great hospitality. Magnetic Island is small—a total of sixteen kilometers of winding, hilly roads bordering the ocean. I do the tour on my motorbike then hike some of the trails. There are a few lovely beaches on the island and at least three backpacker lodges. This little island is the perfect place to get away and relax.

My next big stop is Cairns. The ride continuing north is very pleasant with temperatures of 30 to 32°C. This is tropical country with plenty of palms, fruit trees and continuous blue sky. Winter months, which are just beginning, are comfortably hot, while summer months are extremely hot. I pass several banana plantations and wonder why the stalks of bananas are all wrapped in plastic. Later I learn that they are wrapped to keep the flying foxes and birds from damaging the fruit. I pass through Innisfail and Edmonton before reaching Cairns. I feel like I could be at home—these are names of cities in Alberta.

I contact a cousin of a cousin from British Columbia and stay with them at Clifton Beach for a few days. I have never met Jack and Fran before but they welcome me into their home like an old friend. Fran has just recently retired from a teaching career and Jack will retire in a few weeks. He is a part time musician and plays trombone in a local jazz band in his spare time. Their home is located three blocks from the beach.

As I ride into their driveway Fran meets me and opens the garage door so I can park inside. Then she escorts me to the back of the house to the patio bordering a kidney-shaped pool and a one-bedroom guesthouse. The yard is perfectly manicured and I immediately notice the lipstick palms with their bright red blossoms. Fran shows me into the guesthouse, which will be my home for the next five days.

Two very important items on my to do list are; to make my flight arrangements to Singapore, and to snorkel in the Great Barrier Reef. After that the rest is a bonus.

Early on the morning of May 11 I catch the Quicksilver Coach to Palm Cove Jetty. From here I board the Quicksilver Wave Cutter Catamaran that will take us out to the Great Barrier Reef. I am excited and a bit nervous about this excursion. I'm not a great swimmer and I have only snorkeled twice before in my life. The Catamaran ride lasts about an hour before the captain stops and anchors in a good snorkeling spot. We are given instructions on safety and a mini lesson in snorkeling before donning our equipment and entering the water. Unfortunately the day has become cloudy and snorkeling here does not provide some of the rich colors one usually sees. This tour company pulls a semi-submersible submarine to give tourists another way of viewing the coral reef. When I tire of snorkeling I do the submarine ride—a very enjoyable experience. The boat ride back to Port Douglas is rough and some of the guests are feeling the ill effects of seasickness. I am fine. From Port Douglas I take the coach back to Clifton Beach and give thanks for another wonderful day.

Fran and Jack show me around this beautiful area of northeast Australia. Jack introduces me to some biker friends who belong to the Ulysses Club. Some of the members invite me to do a Sunday ride with their group. On Mother's Day, May 12, I meet the group for breakfast at Ellis Beach. A group of about fifteen riders go north of Cairns as far as Port Douglas and Mossman stopping for breaks at some interesting places. I enjoy the winding roads, great scenery and companionship of these wonderful people. Today has been a great treat.

Monday morning I make some phone calls to book a flight to Singapore. Before I can purchase a one-way ticket I must go to the Singapore Consulate and confirm that they will allow me into the country without a return ticket. Airlines do not like to sell a one-way ticket, it either has to be a return or ongoing to another country. When I bought my ticket from Canada to Australia I had to buy a round trip ticket from Australia to New Zealand so the ticket agency would sell me a one way from Canada to Australia. Since the September 11, 2001, terrorist tragedy in New York, they have become even more strict on this matter. The cost of my plane ticket is $666.00 Australian.

May 15, I leave my new friends Jack and Fran and travel north along the coast to Mossman, stopping at Barron Falls and Barron Gorge. I hike out to a platform overlooking the Gorge. The plank walkways are built high above the rainforest floor and provide a breathtaking view of the gorge and waterfalls that cascade in thin streams to a pool below. This is a great place to take a break and meditate for awhile.

From Mossman I follow the Atherton Tableland south through Mareeba, Atherfort, and Ravenshoe. Rolling hills and pastureland, rainforests, crater lakes, mountain streams and waterfalls make up this magnificent plateau. I have just come across the highest road in Queensland to Ravenshoe, which is the highest town in the province at 930 meters above sea level.

I take the Kennedy Highway and follow the Great Dividing Range as I ride south from Ravenshoe leaving the lush green of the rainforest and entering a dryer climate where plants are scarce and the trees are scraggy and twisted. A few kilometers south of Ravenshoe the road becomes a one-lane bitumen surface down the middle and wide gravel/sand shoulders on each side. The edge of the bitumen drops off sharply and creates its own pattern of scallops and zigzags. I watch attentively for oncoming traffic in the distance, especially for road trains. Road trains are big semi trucks hauling multiple trailers that span up to fifty meters in length. On these roads, and I am sure on any road, they *rule*. They cannot slow down quickly, nor can they leave this narrow strip of bitumen. Several times I slow down to a crawl, drop off the pavement onto the gravel shoulder to let a road train pass before searching for a safe place to ride back onto the pavement. Thankfully it is not raining; I would hate to make these maneuvers on wet ground. At Lynd Junction I turn onto highway 62, which takes me to Charters Towers. The road does not improve. In fact I think it gets worse, if that is possible.

Charters Tower was once the second largest city in Queensland with a population of thirty thousand. Gold was discovered here on December 24, 1871. Now wouldn't that have been the greatest Christmas present ever! In 1887-88 Alexander Malcolm built The Royal Arcade that housed several shops in one building. In 1890 The Royal Arcade became The Charters Towers Stock Exchange. There is a lot of history in this little town that boasts comfortably hot temperatures throughout the whole year.

As I ride west on the Flinders Highway the towns grow farther apart and I find myself once again in the Australian outback. Not much around but wide-open spaces. The terrain is flat and the earth is dry, producing a yellowish brown color. Cattle roam along the roads, as there are no fences.

At Cloncurry the highway changes from Flinders to Barkly Highway as I cross the Selwyn Ranges to Mount Isa. The Selwyn Ranges are rugged red hills contrasted with huge white gum trees. It looks like this area erupted many years ago and dumped the earth in rugged piles to form jagged hills and rocky cliffs. Mount Isa boasts Australia's largest silver, lead, zinc and copper mines and the longest city street in the world. When Mt. Isa incorporated the town of Camooweal situated 188 kilometers to the west, that section of the Barkly Highway became the longest city street in the world. Somewhere along the highway, before reaching Mt. Isa, I read a sign— *You're not an Aussie 'til you've been to Mt. Isa.* Does this make me an Aussie?

Just west of Camooweal I cross into the Northern Territory. From Camooweal to Barkly Homestead is 256 kilometers. I make sure my spare fuel container is full before riding out of town. The landscape is mostly flat red earth or yellow pastureland. Cattle graze freely but I am not sure what they feed on. I see plenty of dead 'roos' along the highway—I seldom see a live one. Still no camels to be seen. I am told there are camels in Australia but I have been almost around the whole continent and into the middle and have not seen one yet. I ride almost seven hundred kilometers today to reach Tennant Creek and decide to stay for a couple of nights. I've been traveling hard for four days since leaving Clifton Beach—it's time to take a break.

I still have a few places I must see and over a thousand kilometers before reaching Darwin. After a good nights sleep and breakfast I pack a little lunch and ride south to Devils Marbles, about 105 kilometers south on the Stuart Highway and approximately four hundred kilometers north of Alice Springs. Devils Marbles Scenic Reserve consists of huge rounded granite boulders, some as large as a house, strewn in jumbled masses across flat ground. Some stand alone, others rest together looking like they could topple over at the slightest touch. But they don't, they stand firm, seemingly resting against each other for support.

To the Aboriginals this a sacred place—*A place of the Dreaming.* I am told that the real stories are not told to the white man, they are known only to the few Aboriginals who need to know. The story told to the visiting public is that this is where women from different tribes gathered to tell their stories of dreaming and to celebrate.

I climb up on a flat surface of a huge boulder and spend some time doing my own dreaming. There is a peaceful and magical feeling here. I pull out my sketchpad and sketch the formation of marbles directly in front of me. What an amazing view—the burnt orange color of the smooth boulders varying in shape and size, make the field look like the work of a sculptor.

Before beginning my hike farther into the field I decide to have a snack. The flies are atrocious and I constantly swat as I walk back to my bike. I take out my banana and continually wave my free hand in the hopes of eating without capturing a fly. These pesky insects are huge and aim for my eyes, ears, nose and mouth. Successful I think! I take out four crackers and try again keeping my free arm swinging. I am on my last bite when I realize, *no flies.* Have they made their way into my mouth un-noticed? In a second, after my free arm stops swinging, one lands on my glasses, another on my ear—that's at least two I haven't eaten!

Back at Tennant Creek I return to the hostel. Across the road is a sign, *Stolen Generation, Resource Council.* In the 1950s and 60s the

Australian Government took Aboriginal children from their families thinking that they were saving the children by putting them in foster care. This so called act of kindness turned out to be a huge mistake. The Resource Council is the Governments way of trying to help families deal with their losses and psychological traumas. I get the feeling it is too little, too late.

This evening I call Servas members David and Norma who live just outside of Katherine. I will make that my stop tomorrow evening.

May 20th I am up early and leave Tennant Creek at 7:30 AM. The air is cool but very comfortable for riding. This is a welcomed reprieve from the heat that will surely come later. At Dunmarra, my second fuel stop for the day, I see a Shell tanker truck at the pumps. He is pulling four tanks—yes *four!* This is the longest road train I have seen. I can't help but study it closely. I count 86 wheels—imagine the cost of rubber on that baby!

The temperature has become very hot, as I knew it would, so I take a couple of extra breaks before reaching Katherine. I locate David & Norma's small farm a few kilometers out of town. David has a rotary meeting tonight so Norma and I spend part of the evening hunting cane toads. Cane toads are unwanted pests. They have a poisonous gland that kills other snakes and animals that happen to eat them. Getting rid of the cane toads is Norma's contribution to controlling the environment and the harm they do. I am not sure how much headway she makes because each night she finds and catches several more.

I leave early next morning for a ride out to Katherine Gorge. I encounter several little wallabies on the road—they tend to come out late at night and very early in the morning. After a most scenic ride to Katherine Gorge, I hike the two-hour loop following the rim of the Gorge. I marvel at the views! On my walk back to the parking area I look up to see thousands of flying fox hanging in the trees. Thank goodness they don't fly in the daylight. The flying fox is like a bat only ten to twenty times bigger. I would not want one of those guys flying over my head.

Back in Katherine I sit in on a "School of the Air" class. Some students live so far away from any center with schools that they are educated by correspondence. Students tune into their class a few hours per week with a teacher using radio communication. The teacher talks to each student, answers their questions, gives assignments and corrects lessons, all by radio. Some of these students live as far as eight hundred kilometers into the outback and this is the only way they can receive an education.

May 22 I continue on to Kakadu National Park where the landscape becomes hilly and somewhat mountainous. I find a hostel in Cooinda and stop early so I can take a boat cruise through the flood lands on Yellow Water and Alligator River. I am able to get a seat on the cruise boat leaving at 4:30, which turns out to be the best time of day to go, as we will be on the water at sunset. We see eight salt-water crocodiles, plenty of birds that inhabit the marsh, and huge beds of water lilies. The reflections in the water are amazing and of course the sun setting over the flood lands is magical. This is one of the greatest highlights of all my travels in Australia.

Next morning I continue on to Border Store and Ubirr at the top end of Kakadu National Park. At Border Store I park my bike and take some crackers out of my top trunk. I have only taken one bite when I am attacked. A big brown bird swoops down and snatches the crackers right out of my hand, and is gone in a flash, leaving scratch marks on my fingers. So much for that little snack!

I leave my bike here and hike out to the Aboriginal Rock Art sites. The carvings in the huge red and grey boulders depict aboriginal life and nature. I continue my hike out to the Ubirr rock formations. Here the rocks have formed in layers creating large, high platforms that overlook the wetlands. I believe this is where one of the very first televised *survivor* challenges was held. I climb up to the top and explore all the interesting crevices and formations.

May 24 I ride into the outskirts of Darwin so I can spend the day making arrangements to ship my bike to Singapore. The first stop on my agenda is the airport. I find it with no problem. Signs for airports and hospitals are always well marked. My flight to Singapore is booked for June 2 and I would like to get the bike flown out a couple of days earlier so it arrives before I do. After a couple of inquiries I am directed to the office of Hellman's Freight Forwarding and introduced to John. I explain that I would like to fly my bike to Singapore. We discuss crating it or not crating it and I push the possibility of strapping it to a pallet without crating. John sends me to another office to talk to Paul. After about an hour of negotiations, Paul agrees to strap it to a pallet for the flight. I am ecstatic! This will save me a lot of money. I am told to bring my bike back on May 30 to prepare it for shipping and go through the Customs check.

I have my bike for another five days so I make the most of getting everything organized and plan some sight seeing events while I still have wheels.

When I leave the airport I contact Servas host Allen Smith, a retired police officer. He has traveling guests from France at the moment but does not hesitate to invite me to stay at his home. I love the chance to meet other travelers. Chris and Evan are from the northern part of France. This is the last few days of their visit in Australia before flying home.

Over the next few days I visit Crocodylus Park where I see crocs over 4.8 meters (15 ft) in length, tour Darwin's Botanical Gardens, an art gallery and museum, hike trails in the well groomed city parks, visit the market next to the beach, shop, and enjoy the company of several servas members. Darwin is a lovely city built on the shores of the Timor Sea, with amazing sunsets and fabulous weather. People are very friendly and relaxed. No one seems to be in a big hurry or pressed for time. I feel at home here.

May 30 I take my bike to Hellman's cargo bay at the airport. I dismantle the windshield, mirrors, and top trunk, drain the fuel, and disconnect and tape the battery cables. They want it as clean as possible so I spent yesterday cleaning it up from top to bottom. The Customs officer has arrived, does an inspection of the bike and verifies the serial number against my *carnet*. He signs the carnet and approves my shipment. I tape and strap all the loose parts onto the bike and ask if I can strap my bike roll on as well. The more I can send with the bike the less I have to take with me on the plane. I am able to stuff all my riding gear, helmet and boots, maps and a host of other things into the roll and strap it to the bike. I strap the empty fuel can onto the right floorboard and the rest is up to Hellman's. This is wonderful! Once again I feel lost leaving my bike in the hands of strangers, but I have to believe that it will arrive in Singapore. I pick up my shipping papers from the office and walk back to Allen's. The cost of flying my bike to Singapore is $899.00 Australian. I am very pleased with that.

Friday I pick up a suitcase from the Red Cross for $2.00. I only need it to get to Singapore, and then I can dispose of it.

Allen has arranged for me to go to Daly River today with the

Blue Lights Disco. The Blue Lights is a volunteer organization run by the police forces throughout all of Australia. They provide dances and discos free of alcohol, drugs and violence for children under the age of eighteen. I am excited and honoured to be a part of it. John, an Aboriginal community police officer, and Lenny (the deejay), pick me up mid afternoon and we drive about 250 kilometers into the outback for this event. Along the way we stop at Adelaide River Inn and Pub. Parts of the movie *Crocodile Dundee* were filmed here and the Water Buffalo used in the film is stuffed and mounted on one end of the bar. We make another stop when we see four Aborigines walking along side of the road holding up an iguana by the tail. The man holding the iguana holds the end of the tail up to eye level and the head almost touches the ground. John tells me they will cook it to eat. I ask John if I can take their picture. He interprets my request and I get a wonderful photo of them holding their prize. They are amazed when I show them the picture on my digital camera.

The Aboriginal name for Daly River is Nauyu (pronounced 'now you'). This is John's hometown and he knows everyone. We set up the instruments in the hall then go for a bite to eat before the disco begins. About 7:30 PM the kids begin to filter into the hall. It does not take them long to get onto the floor and start dancing. Later some of the parents come in and line the walls. Some sit on the few chairs available but most sit cross-legged on the floor. I feel quite out of place. Lenny and I are the minority in this group.

At 10:00, after a wonderful evening of dancing for the kids, we pack up the instruments and head back to Darwin. The drive back is pretty fast. On the straight stretches I notice the speedometer needle sitting at 140 to 150 kilometers per hour. Even at that speed it is a late night getting in.

June 1 I spend the day working on my Web site. Allen has invited some of his friends over for a farewell dinner and we enjoy a great evening visiting. My flight to Singapore leaves at 5:55 tomorrow morning, so I turn in early, as the taxi will be picking me up at 3:45.

Australia is a big country. I have enjoyed my travels *and* the wonderful people I've met. I have put on over eleven thousand kilometers traveling up the east coast from Melbourne to Cairns and across the top end from Cairns to Darwin. What a great ride it has been!

Tomorrow, June 2, I fly to Singapore.

Chapter 7

Singapore — Malaysia

Sunday morning I am up at 3:45 to finish packing and catch a cab to the airport. My flight to Singapore leaves at 5:55. Before boarding I exchange my Australian dollars for Singapore dollars. I am quite surprised that their currency is the dollar. The Australian dollar is only worth 0.9317 Singapore. The Canadian dollar is worth $1.15 Singapore.

My flight takes me to Brunei for an hour layover, arriving at 8:00 AM (9:30 Darwin time). The airport in Brunei is my first experience with *squat toilets*. This is going to be interesting. I can see I am going to have to strengthen those leg muscles.

I arrive at Singapore airport at 11:00—the air is very hot and humid. I have no idea what the temperature is but it must be in the high thirties (Celsius). I have arrangements to stay with servas hosts but will try to get a backpackers room close to the airport for the first night. That would make it easier for picking up my bike tomorrow. I make a few phone calls but don't have any luck unless I want to pay for very expensive accommodations. In the end I decide to call servas hosts, Hans and Lim, and take a cab to their home.

Hans is a young man from Germany married to a beautiful and intelligent Singapore lady. He is tall and slim and has a very serious and sharp mannered personality. Lim is a tiny lady with long black hair and quite soft-spoken. She is very well educated and has a job that takes her traveling to other countries. Hans is an engineer with an excellent job in Singapore.

Hans shows me around and then explains that they are going out this evening but I should make myself at home. Their home is a comfortable flat in a townhouse complex with three bedrooms, a small living room and kitchen, and a small fenced yard with a patio. They rent one larger bedroom to two female students and the third, very small bedroom is where I stay. There is not much soundproofing in the walls that join these homes as I can hear neighbors talking like they were in the next room.

I appreciate the chance to relax and get settled in. Later I take a walk around the area and find a place to have dinner. Food is cheap. I have a huge meal of rice medley with chicken in hot curry sauce served on a soft, flat tortilla shell for $3.50, and a bottle of water for $1.00. The area is full of tightly packed high-rise apartments. Buildings are built close together to make use of every available space of land.

Singapore is a very clean city (country). I say *city* because from what I can tell this little country is *all* city. It has gone from being a tropical rainforest to a concrete jungle. They have even reclaimed land from the ocean and built on that. There are over three million people living in 641 square kilometers. Heavy fines are enforced for littering, so people just don't do it.

Early on the morning of June 3 I make a call to air cargo to enquire about my bike. I am told it will be ready for pickup at SATS cargo tomorrow. My next call is to Singapore Auto Association to find out what regulations I must meet to get my bike on the road. I get the address of the registration and insurance office. Both are in different parts of the city so I study the map carefully before leaving the house.

I catch a bus to China Town and do some sightseeing. The Lonely Planet Guide Book has been a fabulous source of information for finding interesting things to see and do with much of the information coming from other travelers. After lunch I find my way to the Singapore Automobile Association (about an hours walk) and purchase my bike insurance. Then I walk back to Orchard Road, the main shopping district with popular stores, and browse through some of the shops before catching a bus back home.

Singapore people are very tiny and the seats on the bus do not have a lot of legroom. I sit in an aisle seat and have to turn my knees to the side in order to sit—and I am not that tall! I chuckle as I visualize someone as tall as Hans sitting with his knees up around his neck. I watch the people and hear phones ringing all around me. Everyone carries a cell phone. There is no smoking in public places, which is wonderful, but the smell of exhaust hangs heavily in the air.

We pass familiar names like Starbucks, McDonalds, Burger King, Planet Hollywood and many others. Some of the old architecture still remains and is framed by newer hi-rises and skyscrapers built up around them—an interesting mix of old and new mingled together.

I am pleased that I have been able to find my way around in a strange city in a foreign country, use their transportation system, see some of the sights, and find my way back without getting lost. I am not sure what gives me the courage to do this by myself, only that the excitement of the adventure far outweighs the fear.

Next morning I catch a bus to SATS Cargo. The compound covers several blocks and is surrounded with high steel security fence. The security guard in the entrance booth instructs me to get in line for security check and authorization to enter. I take my position in line behind about a dozen other people and absorb everything around me. I soon realize that I am the only woman here. That is a bit unnerving but there is nothing I can do about it so I push the thought out of my mind. Eventually it is my turn and I hand my shipping papers and passport over to the attendant. After passing the *twenty-question-quiz* I am instructed to take the bus around to Cargo Shed 22.

The bus runs regularly through this large compound dropping people off and picking others up at various airline cargo warehouses. Years ago I worked for Canada Post where my job took me to air cargo facilities at the Edmonton International Airport, so I am familiar with airfreight and think this will be a similar experience. Wow, surprise, surprise … I have never seen anything so big! I peer out the window of the bus searching for numbers and names on the many warehouses we pass. I ride for blocks and blocks and begin to wonder if I have missed it. Finally I see number 20 and figure this is a good time to disembark. How am I to know that cargo shed 22 is still several blocks away? I walk for another fifteen minutes before reaching the warehouse where I present my waybill to a lady in the office. She processes the paperwork then points me in the right direction. There is a line on the floor indicating how far customers can go. I take my spot and stand (with several other men waiting to pick up their shipments) scanning this huge warehouse. Forklift drivers whip back and forth moving crates and boxes. I wait and watch as men come and go with their freight in hand. Half an hour elapses, still no bike to be seen. I am feeling a little anxious—this can't be a repeat of my experience in Australia!

I ask one of the warehouse attendants and he tells me they are still getting to it. That does not sound good but all I can do is be patient and wait. Another fifteen minutes passes and still no bike. Finally I take my papers back into the office and ask what the delay is. The lady at the counter is very helpful and calls one of the warehouse officers. They speak in their own language, then the officer motions for me to follow him. Very shortly I see the forklift driver moving a pallet containing a bike secured in shrink-wrap. He deposits it in the middle of the warehouse floor and the officer tells me I can cross the line. He verifies the shipment numbers with my paperwork and asks, "Is there a truck coming to pick this up?"

"No," I reply. "I'm going to unpack it and ride it out."

The poor man looks a bit puzzled so I ask, "Can I unwrap it here?"

He takes a few moments to consider this, and then motions with his hands to the forklift driver to move the pallet slightly off to the side. It is still quite central in the big warehouse and I am allowed to unpack my freight here.

I dig out my little pocketknife and proceed to cut through the layers of shrink-wrap. Hellman's in Australia have done a wonderful job of packaging my bike. Once the shrink-wrap is off and my beautiful Magna is revealed I take out the little tool kit and start re-assembling. I have barely begun laying things out when I notice three young men standing around the bike watching me. Well ... maybe they were eyeing the bike and not me. I can't help but smile as I continue to put the bike back together. No one offers to help, they just watch with interest and big smiles. A few minutes pass before an older gentleman comes over and speaks very quietly to my small audience. The three young men quickly disappear and go back to their work.

It does not take long and I have the bike ready to roll. When I attempt to start it the officer comes over and tells me I cannot start it up in the warehouse. Of course, I should have known that. I ask the officer about the pallet and garbage and he says they will dispose of it. This is great news! In Australia they charged me forty dollars to dispose of the crate. I thank the officer and roll my bike over to the big doors and down the ramp, about a meter to the ground. I am sure every person in the warehouse has stopped working to watch.

Hellman's allowed me to leave about a liter of fuel in the tank so I can start it and ride to a gas station. The bike starts with no problem. I notice that I have an audience standing on the dock. The fellows wear big smiles on their faces and I'm sure they would love to be riding this bike out of here. I think I have gained their respect! I put my riding gear on and give them a wave as I ride to the exit gates. One more security check before I am allowed to leave. All my paperwork checks out and I am set free to explore a whole new world.

A few little reminders sift through my thoughts as I ride out into the streets. Remember to ride on the left—that is my main concern. I am somewhat used to it since Australia, but still not a natural instinct. My first stop is a petrol station, then I make my way to the Land Transport office to obtain an *auto pass* which will allow me to ride on Singapore freeways. I have studied the map well so have no difficulty finding the building. The difficulty starts when I get into the building. I am sent back and forth to several offices before finding someone who knows how to process an auto pass for a foreign motorcycle.

Finally, with highway pass and sticker for my bike in hand, I have everything I need to get on the road. I am cautious as I ride amongst thousands of other vehicles, watching road signs that will lead me back to where I am staying. Traffic is heavy and moving very slowly. I have not been on the road more than twenty minutes when I am bumped from behind. I set my bike on the side stand and get off to take a look. A taxi is behind me and the driver does not seem at all concerned. I am furious and have to fight the urge to kick his lights out! A check of my bike reveals only a bent license plate, so I straighten it out and mutter a few words about his poor driving before mounting up and continuing in what seems to be a traffic jam. Eventually I am out on a major highway and can pick up a bit of speed. It is a bit un-nerving to have an incident so soon after arriving.

June 5—today is my birthday and almost a year since I left home. I have contacted Simon Lee from the *GWRRA Gold Book* and he has invited me to stay with him and his partner Jenny for a few days. Simon comes by to pick me up about 11:30 AM and we go for lunch with his friend Steve. They take me to a restaurant that specializes in western food and I order a Cobb salad—what a great treat! The food is excellent as is the company. Simon and Steve are both riders and very interested in my journey. Simon is in the export business and offers to help with the paperwork for crossing the border into Malaysia.

I have left my bike parked in the little fenced yard at Hans and Lim's townhouse. They are both away for the weekend so I am a bit worried about leaving it there, but Simon assures me the bike will be safe.

Later that evening Simon, Jenny, and their young son Eugene take me out for a traditional Singapore dinner. Patrick, another friend and Goldwing rider, joins us at an outdoor market restaurant. Dinner is a great experience! A large soup pot is placed in the centre of the table on an electric grill. Each of us dish up from a buffet loaded with veggies, fish, chicken, all kinds of seafood and noodles. We place some of the food in the big soup pot to cook and some on a hot platter to grill. Everyone takes what he or she wants from the grill and soup pot, then more food is added and allowed to cook. The meal is excellent! The owner comes out to talk to us after we have finished eating. He is considering taking his restaurant idea to Canada or the USA. I think he has a great product. This evening has been a wonderful birthday gift.

Simon and Jenny have offered me one bedroom in an apartment they lease to students. They tell me I can stay as long as I like. In fact, they suggest that I should stay the week and attend a wedding with them on the weekend. I am tempted but with only motorcycle clothes, boots and runners I would have to go shopping and I really don't have any room on my bike for more clothes. So I politely refuse.

My bedroom is equipped with its own bathroom, TV, stereo and phone. The walls are cement and could use a good paint job, but I have everything I need.

Next day I take a bus down to Little India. The bus drivers speak English and are very helpful. Little India is crowded with shops and people. The shop owners display their wares onto the sidewalk so you must walk right through their shop, and as you do the shopkeeper tries to lure you in to buy. This is what you call high-pressure sales. I am continually saying, "Yes, very nice" and "No thank you." As I stroll in and out of shops I catch the scent of burning incense, of spices and roots, fruits and flowers, all mingling pleasantly together.

The buildings here in Little India are the old architecture of Singapore. When I look in the distance I see newer high-rises surrounding this area creating an interesting contrast—each displaying its own beauty.

For lunch today I stop at a restaurant with no walls on two sides and enjoy the outdoor feeling. I order a vegetarian meal, which is served to me on a banana leaf. The food is delicious and as I eat I notice that people around me are eating with their fingers. Today is very hot and my hands feel quite sweaty—I cannot imagine eating with my fingers! But, as I watch I realize that customers go directly to the sink at the back of the restaurant to wash their hands before they sit down. I must try this custom another time.

Next morning Simon picks me up at 10:30 and we drive across the border into Malaysia. Simon is in the export business and has an office in Johor. He tells me he wants to make sure I know where to go tomorrow and that I have no trouble crossing the border with my bike. He speaks to the customs officer and explains the carnet. We leave feeling comfortable that I will have no problems crossing, and then continue on to Johor.

Simon has some business to take care of so I wait for him in the reception office where about twelve people work. I ask directions to the toilet and am shown through the busy office to the back. The facilities are fancy with a squat toilet and shower in each stall and several chrome knobs lining the wall. I cannot read the labels etched on each knob so have no idea which one flushes the toilet. Oh well, I'll just try them all. I turn the first knob and instantly I am wet! My hair is wet, my t-shirt is wet, and my slacks are wet! Now what am I going to do? I have to walk back through the office full of employees and I am sure Simon will be back soon. How am I going to explain this? Well, I cannot stay in here forever. I'm just going to walk out there like nothing is wrong and hope that no one notices. A few eyes turn in my direction as I walk through the office and take my seat in the reception area. The temperature is in the high thirties so maybe my t-shirt will dry before Simon returns. What an embarrassing moment!

On our way back to Singapore, Simon asks if I have bike insurance for Malaysia. He informs me that I can get it in Singapore and takes me to AAS (Automobile Association Singapore), where I was just a couple of days ago, to extend my insurance. The cost is one hundred and three

Singapore dollars, which Simon pays and refuses to let me pay him back. These people are so good to me. After a wonderful dinner with Simon and his family at a high class Chinese Restaurant, we stop for coffee with some fellow Goldwing riders. The guys present me with a can of chain lube, helmet spray and windshield polish. They are in awe of my journey and would love to be doing the same thing.

On the way home Simon stops at a 7/11 store to top up my auto pass. I want to stop at a bank machine to pay him back for the insurance and now the auto pass, but he will not hear of it. I feel extremely grateful and blessed to have met these wonderful people.

June 8 I leave Singapore and cross the border into Malaysia. Simon comes by at 8:00 AM and we go for a traditional breakfast of pancakes made Singapore style. The batter is a yogurt base and spread thin to form a pancake thirty centimeters in diameter, which is fried on a griddle, folded twice to form a triangle and served with three spicy sauces. Very tasty—the only thing that could make it better would be our Canadian maple syrup.

After breakfast we pick up my bike. En route Simon stops at a bank machine and takes out one hundred and thirty ringgit (Malaysian money). When he hands it to me I protest—this is about sixty Singapore dollars. He insists I take it. I am so overwhelmed! How can I ever repay him?

I ride back to the apartment, pack my gear then follow Simon to the main highway leading to the border. I am feeling comfortable about this border crossing. Simon has shown me the lane to use—the one only bikes go through. When I arrive there is a whole pack of bikes in line—mostly 100 to 150cc bikes used to go back and forth to work. A lot of people cross the border to work in Malaysia. I pull in line behind at least fifty bikes with more rolling in steadily behind me. It does not take me long to realize I have to be aggressive to hold my spot as small bikes crowd in and push past me. Okay guys, if that's the game, I can play too. I keep edging my front tire into the slightest opening and soon bikes from behind are no longer crowding me out. As unfamiliar as this action is to me I know that if I am to survive I must *do as the natives do*.

About a forty-five minute wait in line and it is my turn at the wicket. I hand over my passport and carnet, am asked a few customary questions, the clerk *chops* my documents and I am back in line to enter

Malaysia customs. This is a faster line and soon my documents are chopped again and I am set free to travel in Malaysia. My passport stamp indicates I have three months. I do not plan to be here that long but it is important to check and know how much time they have given me.

You might remember that Malaysia was not one of the countries included on my *carnet de passage* due to the high import tax. I am very fortunate to have met Simon and have him intervene for me. The universe certainly does provide for all our needs—in ways we can never know or plan for.

I stay on the main highway for about eighty kilometers before turning west on highway 96 to reach highway 5, which follows the west coast almost to Thailand. The main highway, which runs north and south through Malaysia, is a four lane divided highway with perfectly manicured boulevards between and along both sides. The vegetation is green and lush, there is no litter to be seen, and the pavement is relatively new and a joy to ride on. Simon suggested I stay on this highway all the way, but I am set on seeing the coastline.

Once I reach highway 5 I understand why Simon suggested I stay on the freeway. This route takes me through many small towns that seem like one continual market of open stalls filling the streets. I share the highway with cars, trucks, lorries (beat up old trucks hauling their product), motorbikes, bicycles, and more. I notice motorbikes riding on the left shoulder, so I follow suit whenever it looks safe. On several occasions the shoulder is the only way around stopped or slow moving traffic.

When I reach Batu Pahat I stop at a big shopping mall for lunch. The mall is very noisy and I am surprised to see KFC, Pizza Hut, MacDonald's and many other familiar names. I do not linger long as my bike is parked in the public parking lot with all my gear on it. The only thing I take with me is my tank bag—it contains some valuable items and would be too easy to steal. The noise in the mall, from music and the hum of conversation, is horrendous and I wonder how people can tolerate it.

I eat quickly and return to my bike. Everything is as I left it. The temperature is in the high thirties and the air very humid. Putting my riding jacket back on requires a lot of effort but I do not dare ride without it—the traffic out there is not what I am used to. I make my way back onto highway 5 en route to Melacca. The landscape all the way is hilly and green with lots of trees including palms and numerous kinds of fruit trees. It's a pretty area, but traveling is slow going.

I reach Melacca about 4:00 PM and begin looking for the Kancil Guest House. This place was highly recommended by servas members I met in Singapore. I have the address and it looks like it should be easy to find. I ride around for an hour, stopping and asking several people for directions, before finally spotting it. The front of the guesthouse is on a very narrow, busy street that has no room for parking. I find a little driveway about a block away, park my bike and walk back to the building.

The front door to the Guest House is locked so I ring the buzzer. I wait a couple of minutes—no answer. Press the buzzer again and wait. Finally a lady comes to the door. I ask about a room and yes, she can accommodate me.

"Where do I park my bike?" I ask.

"Ride down that trail," she says as she points in the direction of my bike, "and I will meet you in the back and unlock the gate."

That sounds promising. I like the fact that her yard is locked. I return to my bike and follow a trail through tall grass, ruts, rock and mud. At one point I almost lose control but a little twist on the throttle pulls me out of the mud hole and over a sharp ridge before reaching the gate. The fence is at least eight feet tall, covered in trees, shrubs and flowers, and surrounds a large ground level patio and well-kept, private yard. As I ride in I see three other bikes parked on the patio. This is great! I pull my bike up behind them and proceed to unpack.

I am given a room on the ground floor, which is one of five that surround a central garden patio. The garden area is a sitting room with a little pond and fountain, trees, flowers, tall vases and ornaments scattered throughout. What a lovely spot. I can see that this is where I will be doing my journal writing. My room is at the end adjoining the garden and closest to the kitchen. The bedrooms are very basic with cement outer walls and thin-boarded inner walls that stop about half a meter from the ceiling. Only one wall of my room borders the next bedroom. I am a bit concerned that a person could climb that wall quite easily and be in my room. Fatima, the owner, assures me I will be safe, "but keep everything locked up," she adds.

I carry in everything I want from the bike and get settled, then have a cup of tea with Fatima. She seems like a friendly lady. Her husband is away working and she runs the guesthouse. Shortly, three guests come into the kitchen from the back patio. I am introduced to Jen and Marten from Holland and John from Switzerland. They are the owners of the bikes parked out back. Marten rides a BMW R1100GS, Jen is a new rider and rides the BMW F650GS and John rides the Yamaha XT550. I am so excited to meet them. We all go out for dinner and hit it off like we were long time friends.

Sunday morning I am up early sitting in the garden area working on my computer when Fatima gets up. She opens the back door and calls to me "come see." I grab my camera expecting to see a pretty bird or interesting creature, instead I see the saddlebags on my bike wide open and the contents scattered out on the lawn.

Fatima immediately goes to wake John and Marten and Jen; while I start taking pictures of my bike and belongings. My new riding boots that I just purchased in Australia are gone, my electric pant liners, first aid kit, international electrical plugs and other small items I have not yet realized—all gone. By this time Marten and Jen have determined that their new Compaq laptop they bought four weeks ago is gone, along with numerous other articles. I am thankful I had taken my laptop into my room and locked it in my removable top trunk.

The locks on my saddlebags were useless. They did not even get damaged in the break-in. Marten and Jen have metal panniers with strong locks, which were both damaged. They will have to replace the locks and do some major straightening to the panniers to make them usable. Both panniers were broken into on Marten's bike and one on Jen's. John's bike was not touched. It was parked closest to the building and we surmise that the thieves left once they found the computer, or were scared off before they got to his bike.

Needless to say we are all very upset. We walk to the police station to submit a report. The officers do not seem too interested but we persist until someone takes this seriously. Finally they take our report and tell us they will send an officer out to take pictures. We do not expect to recover anything but at least the police are aware of the incident.

We stay close to the guesthouse for the remainder of the day. That evening, after checking our e-mail, Jen announces she is taking us all out for dinner. She has made some money on stocks her broker sold for her today and she wants to celebrate. What excellent news to end off a day that began with such a shock.

We all sleep lightly this night. In the morning over breakfast we share that each of us were up twice in the night and looked out the door to check on the bikes. Not one of us encountered the other—we laugh and determine that we did a good night of surveillance.

June 10, I remember my mother's birthday. She is eighty-five today. My thoughts go back to my last visit with her before I left on my trip. I told her I would be gone for a couple of years traveling around the world. I omitted the fact that I would be traveling by motorcycle so as not to alarm her. Her memory has been failing for several years now so I am not sure how much her mind could comprehend, or if she would remember our conversation once I left. Mom worked hard all her life and I believe there wasn't anything she could not do. She taught me to be independent and it was her example that gave me the will and courage to do the things I have done in life. I thank her for that and am so glad she had a chance to travel before her health began to fail.

After breakfast we go for a walk through the old city. We arrive at the visitor information in the heart of the historic Dutch area when the sky opens up and pours rain for fifteen minutes. It comes down so hard and fast that it leaves puddles as deep as our ankles. The rain stops as quickly as it started and the sun comes out creating a beautiful hot day.

My sightseeing companions head for the guesthouse after about an hour—they have work to do on their bikes. I continue to explore the old city. The streets are narrow, cramped with shops with their product displayed right to the edge of the sidewalk. The buildings are old but preserved to retain their history. I pop in and out of shops wishing I had the money to buy souvenirs and ship them home. Oh well, just as well. I can't possibly buy things from every place I visit. I pass by Kampung Kling's Mosque—one of the oldest mosques in the country, Hang Jebat's Mausoleum, several churches, museums, a Dutch graveyard and several other old buildings constructed in the 17th and 18th centuries. I come to an area that looks like China Town. Shops are packed with every kind of craft you can imagine. As I leisurely stroll through the streets I recognize smells of fruit, flowers, incense, spice, and much more that I do not recognize. Gutters line the edges of the streets and sidewalks go a step up then a step down. I stub my toe several times before I learn to watch where I am walking. Cars, trucks, motorcycles and bicycles jam the narrow streets passing within inches of each other. I wonder if I will ever get used to vehicles passing so close they almost brush my hip and shoulder!

Melaka, or Malacca as it is known today, was founded in the late thirteen hundreds by a Sumatran Prince. It is believed that he named the area after the *melaka* tree he was resting under. Melaka prospered and grew bigger and bigger progressing into a booming international trade post. In the later fourteen hundreds it caught the attention of the Europeans, eventually being conquered by the Portuguese. In 1641 the Dutch captured Melaka from the Portuguese. Today the Dutch history is still very apparent.

Surrounding the old city of Melaka is the new city filled with high-rises, apartments, office buildings and nearly five hundred factories. The state has poured billions of ringgit into factories creating over eighty thousand jobs. Their products are diverse, ranging from rubber gloves, footwear to computer parts. Malaysia has a 20/20 vision—that is to achieve developed country status by year 2020. Current projections are to develop Malacca into a manufacturing haven to help the country achieve their goal.

Jen and Marten have invited me to ride with them. I graciously accept and am thrilled to have riding companions for a few days. Today we are heading to Kuala Lumpur. Marten has a GPS mounted on his bike so I am very happy to follow and let him do the navigating. We stay on the coastal route, highway 5 heading north. Riding is slow going as we pass through many small villages and towns and some resorts along the Strait of Malacca. The terrain is hilly, green with trees and other vegetation. We pass perfectly manicured palm tree plantations where palms are harvested for their oil. We ride by a pasture with a herd of cows so skinny you can count their ribs.

Traffic on this road is busy. Small motorbikes carrying three and four people seem to be the norm here. Usually Mamma and Papa are wearing helmets, t-shirts, pants and flip-flops or sandals on their feet. The children, tucked in between the adults, wear t-shirts, shorts and no shoes or helmets. Many sights we are not accustomed to. Imagine passing two motorbikes riding together, front wheel of the back rider in line with the back wheel of the front rider. The rider on the back bike has his foot, clad only in a flip-flop, positioned on the end of the exhaust pipe of the front bike. We discover later that this is how they push a bike that is broke down or out of gas.

We finally reach Kuala Lumpur and find our way to the Hotel Fujisan, which we choose because of recommendations from other bikers. The rooms are pretty basic but they have underground, locked parking—that is worth the price of 68 ringgit. Imagine our surprise when the clerk asks how many hours we want the room for. We are a bit shocked considering other bikers recommended this hotel. The clerk quickly gives us the *other* rate, the *per night* rate. I guess they cater to both types of clients.

For the next week we walk the streets of Kuala Lumpur, sightseeing, shopping, trying new foods, taking pictures and having a lot of laughs. I am thoroughly enjoying the company of my new friends. I will miss them immensely when we split up.

Malaysia has many cultures, the most prominent being the ancient Malay culture, Chinese and Indian. China and India have been the most prominent trading partners throughout history. Most Malays are Muslim. With the migration of Chinese and Indians came Buddhism and Hinduism. A thousand years later, with the arrival of Arabs, Islam was introduced. All these cultures mingle in the streets of KL

I am in awe of the modern architecture. The skyline is spotted with some of the most impressive towers I have seen anywhere. The most striking of all is the Petronas Towers—KL's Twin Towers. The steel and glass exterior of the Towers glistens in the sun as they rise 452 meters into the sky. At the time of completion it was the highest building in the world boasting eighty-eight stories, 213,750 square meters of usable space and five thousand square meters of parking. The bridge connecting the two towers is on levels forty-one and forty-two, at 171 meters above sea level. We take the elevator to the bridge deck and are rewarded with the most spectacular view of the city and the gardens below. The structure is surrounded by incredible gardens, statues, pools with dancing water fountains, trees and flowers, and walking paths with benches—truly magnificent!

There is no shortage of shopping complexes in KL. Malls and shopping towers go on for blocks and blocks. Electronics shops are plentiful. I end up buying a palm pilot, keyboard and case. This will be handy for keeping my journals and I can download them onto my computer. During one of our shopping days I look for shoe protector spray. Jen and I ask at every shop we enter and each time we are sent in a different direction. One shop owner points down the hall and says, "You go that way, you find it somewhere." We have to stifle our laughs until we are out of hearing range. I guess they would rather tell us something than admit they do not know.

Martha, a friend of Jen's, has joined them for a two-week holiday. She will ride as a passenger behind Marten. Today, June 17, John arrives in KL. We all go for dinner and catch up on stories since we parted in Malacca.

The following morning we have breakfast at Starbucks before saying goodbye to John again and leaving for Bukit Fraser (Bukit means *hill* or *mountain*). It takes awhile to get out of KL. We encounter roadblocks and detours and once again I am thankful to be following Marten with his GPS. I really should learn how to use one, but right now is not the time.

Our first stop is the Batu Caves, which were discovered by an American naturalist over 120 years ago. We park the bikes and take off our heavy riding coats and pants. Jen has decided to stay with the bikes so we have the luxury of leaving our gear. The entrance to Temple (or Cathedral) Cave, the largest of the Batu Caves, is 272 steps leading upwards and into the cavities of the limestone hill. We stop at little caves along the way before reaching Temple Cave. The entrance is framed with towering limestone formations and inside, at the centre, stands a Hindu Shrine. Many old statues can be seen carved into the walls of the cave all the way up to the top. Macaque monkeys living in the caves scamper and swing all around us. They perch on the heads of statues and are always on the lookout for food.

Back on the bikes we ride north on highway 68 to Genting Highlands, an exquisite resort city built on the top of a hill two thousand meters above sea level and only fifty kilometers from Kuala Lumpur. Lush green tropical rainforest covered in a veil of mist envelops the hills surrounding this little city of four and five star hotels, high end shopping and restaurants, theme parks, the country's only casino, and numerous recreation facilities. All this luxury combined with the crisp clean mountain air, incredible scenery, temperatures ranging from 16 to 23°C, and reprieve from the heat, dust and noise of KL is what brings people here to this luxurious hilltop resort. We simply ride through and continue on down the hill. The budgets of long-distance bikers does not allow for this kind of luxury.

We descend the spiral road back to highway 68 then take highway 8 north for about ninety kilometers. The smoothly paved road winds around mountains clad in thick jungle. Little shrines pop up periodically just off the side of the road. There is enough room to pull off the road and say prayers or leave offerings for the Gods. We stop at one shrine to take pictures and I silently hope we are not being disrespectful. We reach the junction of highway 8 and 55 where we turn west onto a much narrower road with tight, twisty curves leading to Bukit Fraser. In a few kilometers we reach a control gate. The time is 4:40 PM—we have another eight kilometers to ride before reaching the summit, but the gate is closed and we are informed that we must wait until 5:00 to go up. This stretch of the road is one lane with uphill traffic limited to odd hours and downhill traffic to even hours.

We do not have long to wait but the day is hot so we throw our jackets over our bikes and sit on the curb and relax. Motorbikes are allowed to come to the front of the line so we will be the first ones out the gate. Jen will go first, me second and Marten last. We have decided on this order because Marten and Jen both have intercoms and I don't. We are told that this stretch of road is very narrow and twisty, clinging to the side of the mountain as it climbs in elevation.

119

We watch as a few vehicles come down through the gate, as we wait patiently for 5:00 o'clock. We are geared up and ready to roll as soon as the gate opens. Jen is a little nervous but does just great. We climb another six hundred meters in eight kilometers to reach the summit at 1,524 meters above sea level. Bukit Fraser is another little resort village built at the top of the hill. There are a few hotels, condo units, a hostel, store, café, post office and golf course. Many good walking trails through the jungle, bird watching and a beautiful golf course attract local and foreign visitors alike.

We take a little tour around before stopping at Silvertip Resort to check the price of their condo units. The owner speaks French and Jen is able to negotiate a deal. For a two-bedroom unit with kitchen, living room, patio, and two bathrooms, including breakfast for four—210 ringgit per night. In Canadian dollars, less than twenty-two each. For my Dutch friends carrying Euros, the deal is exceptional!

I am up at 5:30 next morning to relax on the patio and watch the sun rise. My riding companions still sleep and I engulf the solitude. The temperature is cool enough that I wear long sleeves. Our condo sits high on the hill and from the patio I look out over the jungle. The sun has not yet risen and a mist hangs over the tops of the trees. All is quiet except for the call of the monkeys far below in the jungle and the occasional song from a bird. As the sun starts to show itself over the hills I think to myself, *this is heaven.* I want to capture the moment and hold it forever.

When my companions appear we go for breakfast then do a walking tour of Bukit Fraser. Early afternoon John arrives and we welcome him like family. An afternoon walk in the jungle proves exciting as we spot monkeys playing in the trees. There is just something special about seeing wild animals in their natural habitat.

Next morning I am up early again—seems I do not want to miss a moment of time I have here. John is sleeping on the living room floor so I tiptoe past him and quietly open the door to go out for a walk. I turn to go down the step and right in my path is the biggest insect I have ever seen! He is at least the size of a mans hand, with a hard shell, three steel like horns protruding up and six long legs with dangerous looking claws at the ends. I am not sure if I should step past him or turn back to the door. What if he attacks me? I don't want to wake anyone up this early, so I cautiously step around him and race down the remaining three steps. I hope he is not there when I return from my walk.

I walk for about an hour and when I return the creature is still on the step. John is up by now and I call him out to see. He doesn't know the name of this guy but does know that if you pick it up by its hard shell it cannot hurt you. I run and get my camera and take a picture. Later I e-mail the picture to Liam, my six-year-old grandson and bug specialist. If anyone will know what it is, Liam will. Sure enough, next time I check my e-mail I have an answer.

"Grandma, that's a rhinoceros beetle," he writes.

Well of course, I should have known that! I am so proud of my grandson.

Once everyone is up we pack our bikes before going for breakfast. Today we will ride to Cameron Highlands, which is about 145 kilometers north, and over fifteen hundred meters above sea level. You would think 145 kilometers would only take an hour and a half. No so! The tight curves, narrow roads and busy villages along the way keep us from getting up any speed.

I take the lead today, Jen second, Marten and Martha third and John brings up the rear. Jen, being a new rider, is still very nervous on the tight curves and narrow roads. We take our time and watch carefully for trucks, busses and the odd car drifting over the centerline. We take Highway 1 north to Tapah then the narrow, winding highway 59 to Tanah Rata. Tanah Rata is a popular spot in the Highlands for visitors wanting to enjoy the cooler weather and trekking in the jungle. This area is Malaysia's largest tea producing region. Tea plantations covering the hills provide a luxurious manicured landscape. Strawberry patches, Rose gardens, vegetable farms, a butterfly farm and Chinese temples are just some of the other attractions here.

We search out Father's Guesthouse and find they are almost full. John takes a room here and the rest of us continue looking. We find two spacious rooms available at Cameronian Guesthouse for fifty ringgit each—what a great deal! The room Martha and I take has a queen size bed and bunk beds. There is a delightful, quiet, garden patio off the side where we relax for an hour before calling on John for dinner.

About 6:30 this evening we walk up the hill to Father's Guesthouse. John introduces us to Jason, a world traveler from England. Jason rides a BMW 1100GS, same as Martens. We walk into town and find an

Indian restaurant. Tonight we are all game to try the custom of eating with our fingers. We are told that you eat with your right hand *only;* to use your left is unclean. Eating with your fingers is not as easy as you may think. It takes some practice chasing rice, veggies and sauce around the banana leaf (which incidentally lacks sides to help trap the food) with your fingers, and carry it to your mouth without spilling it down the front of your shirt. Regardless, we have a great time, laugh a lot, and attract some curious glances from the locals.

John is from Switzerland. He is about forty-five years old, short and slim, with a full head of black hair, a mustache and always has a smile on his face. Jason is completely opposite, except for the smile. He is in his mid twenties, about 5 feet 10 inches tall with sandy blond hair. Over the course of the evening we discover that Jason has retinitis pigmentosis—more commonly known as RP. RP is a degenerative eye disease causing blindness, commonly striking late teens and young adults. His brother is already going blind and Jason knows he will also lose his sight. He is traveling the world now while he can still see. My heart aches for this young man and at the same time I admire his outlook on life. He has a great sense of humor and lives life to the fullest.

The next morning John, Martha and I join some other guests on a guided hike. Our guide, Allan takes us on trail number ten to Gunung Jasar at eighteen hundred meters above sea level. The Climb is strenuous but we are rewarded with a wonderful view once we reach the top. We look out over the trees and can see all the way to Tanah Rata, where we are staying, and Brichang, another little town in the hills. The trek back is much easier as we head mostly down hill. Part way down the trail the soles of my new boots, just purchased in KL, come loose at the toes. A few steps more and they are flapping like duck feet. I cannot possibly finish the hike like this, nor can I take them off. I start to watch for anything on the ground that I can use to tie the sole onto the boot. My trekking companions are having a good laugh at my predicament. I manage to find a piece of twine and tie up one sole. Hey, this works just great! I pick up a strong, thin vine and fix the other boot. This should get me back to the guesthouse.

A short time later we descend to Orang Asli, a little native Indian village. Small square houses, some with little decks, dot the hillside surrounded by forest. No paint covers the dry brown boards. Clothes hang on lines extending from the houses. Children play and laugh in one big open yard and wave as we walk by. The village resonates a feeling of calm and peace.

A few more steps and the vine tied to my left boot wears through. I find another one and re-tie it. I will have to do this twice more before reaching the guesthouse.

We pass Pirat Falls as we continue down. The river is very dirty with old clothes and debris caught on branches floating down the river. This country is so beautiful, it is such a shame there is no litter control. Farther down we pass All Souls Church. I like that name. Then we are back in Tanah Rata. I break from the group and go in search of a store to buy glue. Hopefully I can fix my boots.

By the time I reach the guesthouse my left sole is flapping again. I saunter up the path with a slap—clomp, slap—clomp, slap—clomp. Jen is sitting in the garden reading and raises her head wondering what that noise is. When she spots my boots she nearly falls off her chair laughing.

Next morning the six of us, Marten, Jen, Martha, John, Jason and I, go sightseeing with the bikes. Our first destination is Gunung Brinchang at 2,031 meters. We climb the lookout tower and enjoy a vast view of the tea plantations, strawberry farms, and more nestled amongst the forests and jungles. Next stop is Sungai Palas Tea Plantation where we do a tour of the plant before stopping for tea and cake at their restaurant.

The view from the patio overlooks a valley of perfectly lined rows of tea trees with poinsettia trees in full bloom lining one side and palm trees in bloom scattered here and there. Another one of those peaceful settings I will record in my memory and cherish forever.

As we continue our ride we cannot drive past the strawberry farm without stopping. They also sell vegetables and John, being the health nut, buys carrots. Jen and I buy strawberries and chocolate. The last stop for the day is the Sam Poh (Buddhist) Temple situated high on a hill overlooking the town of Brinchang. This large, ornately designed temple houses several large, gold plated Buddhas and other Statues. I will see many more like this as I travel through Asia.

Today has been a fun-filled day sightseeing with my friends. Jason has a great sense of humor and keeps us laughing continually, John never loses his smile, Marten and Martha are the serious ones, and Jen and I never stop laughing. You would think we have known each other for years. I enjoy their company immensely.

Next day we do a ten-kilometer hike up to the top of Cameron

Highlands—a strenuous climb for people like us who much prefer to ride than walk. But some places are just not accessible by motorcycle. The tracks through the jungle are rough with massive root systems to stumble over, narrow trails and gullies just wide enough to put one foot in front of the other. Occasionally we are blessed with a level track with a soft under-cushion of leaves. It is heaven while it lasts.

June 24 Jen, Marten, Martha and I start out for Taman Negra National Park. After about 310 kilometers of tight curves and over 30°C heat we escape to the expressway for about seventy kilometers. The sides of the expressway are kept impeccably clean. I marvel at this after riding secondary roads that succumb to a great deal of litter. We are exhausted by the time we reach Jerantut on the junction of highway 64 and 92. We decide to stop for the day and get rooms across the road from the police station for thirty ringgit. One problem though—they do not have secured parking, so we ride to the police station and ask permission to park our bikes inside their fenced compound. We can sleep easy tonight.

Today I bought two thousand Nortel shares for $2.60 per share. The stock has been continually going down for the past year. Over the past year I bought them at $9.00 and $5.60 share. I have a feeling it has to turn around soon. (**Note:** February, 2004, I sold my Nortel shares for just over $11 a share.)

We do not have far to go today so we are in no hurry to get on the road. We are taking a road that is not even on the map, but will take us to Taman Negra National Park.

We travel very slowly and I find myself getting irritable. If I had been riding alone I would have made this stretch yesterday. We encounter about four kilometers of construction with stretches of big, thick rocks on the road. A bit un-nerving, but we all make it through without incident. We finally reach Kuala Tahan, just outside the park, and find accommodation at Teresek View Motel. Once again Jen bargains with the owner and succeeds in getting us two cabins at forty ringgit each (down from sixty). Our little cabins, situated on a tree lined dirt street, are painted brightly with burgundy exterior walls, a soft green door and window frames, and blue trim below the red corrugated, tiled roof. Very colorful! We are able to park our bikes right outside our door.

We have about half a kilometer to walk downhill to reach the Tahan River, which divides us from Taman Negra National Park. No vehicles are allowed in the park. Six or seven small wood buildings float on platforms along the edge of the river. They are rectangular in shape with a covered dining patio at one end and a kitchen at the other. To access the restaurant we have to walk a thirty-centimeter wide plank, four to five meters long, connecting the rocky shore to the building. We are careful to keep our balance as we cross.

After lunch we take a long tail boat (like a long canoe) across the river and buy our park pass for six ringgit. We do a short walk down to a swimming hole and wade in. The water is yellowish-brown looking but clear enough to see to the bottom. This is a warm and a refreshing treat after a hot sweaty ride.

Back at Kuala Tanah, Martha and I take a walk through the village and come across some interesting rental huts made from wood and straw—a little more basic than the ones we are booked into.

Everyone moves at a slow pace here. No hustle and bustle like we see at home—people rushing hurriedly to and from work, to and from school, hockey practice, ball, soccer, figure skating, dance and all the other things we cram into our lives. We discover the big excitement for this evening is the football game between Germany and Korea being televised. Two of the floating restaurants have TV's suspended from the ceiling so for dinner we walk down and join the action. The restaurant is packed with local men bursting with excitement in anticipation of the upcoming game. We meet another group of travelers from Holland and my friends have a great time exchanging greetings from home.

The next two days we spend trekking in the jungles of Taman Negra National Park. We do a strenuous climb on a trail that leads us to the Canopy Walk. The fee is five-ringgit to cross seven suspension bridges swinging high amongst the treetops, and suspended by cables tied to trees. It claims to be the longest in the world at five hundred meters. The tallest point above the jungle floor is forty-five meters. On this stretch only four people are allowed on the bridge at one time. We are instructed to stay ten meters back from the person in front and can gauge our distance by the markers on the bridges. The bridge floor consists of thirty-centimeter wide planks laid end to end on a ladder-like structure placed into rope webbing. This webbing wraps around and comes up about two-thirds of a meter on both sides to form the side handrails. Ropes placed at about one-meter intervals attach the handrail to a wire cable strung between platforms. It feels pretty shaky at times but the view of the jungle floor from here is superb. After the bridges we continue to Bukit Teresik. The climb is steep and difficult. We stumble and tramp over huge root systems exposed across the track—definitely different than New Zealand trails. The jungle displays an amazing beauty with roots and vines twisted and looped to resemble artist sculptures. Hundreds of shades of green, a gazillion shaped leaves and the occasional flower makes us stop to capture it in a picture.

We reach the top of Bukit Teresik, stop and enjoy the view before descending on tracks steeper and more treacherous than before. By the time we reach level ground we have walked for four hours and are soaked with perspiration. Even the beak of my cap drips moisture in front of my eyes. Regardless, this has been a most challenging and fabulous day.

Next morning the restaurants are a little farther out in the river. It rained hard overnight and the water is high. Restaurant owners have laid additional planks down to get to their doors. Wow! If we thought the planks were shaky before, we really have to use our balance this morning. We all make it across without falling in, have breakfast and cross to the park for our last day in the jungle.

Today our trek takes us up to Gua Telinga Caves. Jen, Martha and I are sure we do not want to go into the caves, so this trek is for Marten. Bats, snakes and who knows what other creatures occupy the caves. Besides, the spaces in some parts are so small you have to crawl through on your stomach! Just before reaching our destination we meet Rob, from New Zealand, heading in the same direction. Wonderful ... now Marten has someone to explore the caves with.

The track is steeper than yesterday and in some places guide ropes are attached so you can pull yourself up. In other places ropes are tied between trees as a guardrail on the cliff side. The trail down is even more rugged. Near the jungle floor we encounter thick heavy vines hanging from the trees like a giant swing. Needless to say, the child in us comes out to play. We climb on the vines and swing in the jungle like Tarzan. I am sorry to see this trek come to an end.

June 28 we leave Kuala Tanah at 9:00 AM and travel together back to Benta. We stop for lunch then say our goodbyes through tears. We have traveled together for almost three weeks and find it tough to part. But part we must. My friends are heading south to Indonesia and I, north to Thailand.

I continue north on highway 8 to Gua Masung, riding through mountainous and jungle terrain. Many towering, jagged rocks poke up on either side of the road creating a unique countryside. The few homes scattered along the route are mostly brown wooden shacks. When I reach Gua Musang I find Kesadar Inn that was recommended by another biker. The price is eighty-six-ringgit for a standard room.

Outrageous! I negotiate the price down to seventy-one—still way more than I want to pay, but I take it anyway.

I am on the road earlier next morning. No more lazing around, I will resume my schedule of riding early to beat some of the heat.

My destination is Gerik and my map shows a perfectly good road going across the mountains directly north of Gua Masung, cutting off several kilometers. It connects to highway 4 which is a main highway leading right into Gerik. The first town, about half way across is Dabong. The road starts out newly paved with wide shoulders. After several kilometers it becomes a narrow strip of pavement, but still smooth and good riding. Then abruptly the pavement ends and I am on rough gravel/rock/dirt road. I ride a few meters and the road quickly gets worse. I can see a work crew ahead so I ride to them and try to ask how far this construction goes. Well, of course they do not understand me but their hand signals indicate that I should turn back. When I point in the direction I want to go they frantically wave their arms and shake their heads 'no, no, no.' It seems I have no choice but to retrace the fifty kilometers I have just ridden. Back I go to Gua Masung thinking, *I should have listened to the monk who told me not to take that road.* Before I left the parking lot earlier this morning I spoke (well sort of spoke, mostly it was sign language) with a monk staying at the motel. When I showed him the map and the road I wanted to take he shook his head and waved his arms, much like the construction workers did. He pointed to grass and gravel, even bent down and picked up some earth; but I thought—"He's probably never been more that fifty kilometers out of Gua Musang, what would he know."

I retrace my route, ride past Gua Masung and take the main highway around the long way to Kuala Krai. About forty kilometers out of K Krai I see another sign to Dabong. This time the sign is very clear, Dabong 43 kilometers, so I figure it must go through from this side. Again the road is newly paved with very little traffic and gentle curves winding through the mountains, jungle and rainforest. At thirty-three kilometers the pavement quits! Now I'm thinking that with only ten kilometers to go I will continue. About a kilometer into an awful road of rock, gravel, potholes, broken pavement and mud holes I start to get nervous. I have heard about the bandits that hide out in the hills and here I am alone in the mountains on a road from hell. I am simply too stubborn to turn around—or maybe too afraid I will drop my bike in this mess if I try to make a U-turn. I continue riding and after four kilometers I am back on pavement. Great!

When I arrive at the town site my first mission is to find a petrol station. Dabong is a little mountain village with small wooden houses and shops cramped together on narrow dirt streets. I am surprised to discover a train track running through these mountains. I stop a few times and try to ask directions to a gas station but no one understands me. Finally, after pointing franticly to my gas tank, a pleasant old gentleman waves down two young fellows on a scooter and one of them can understand and speak a little English. He points me in the direction of a petrol station (which I never do find) and then tells me the road continuing across to highway 4 does not exist.

"It hasn't been built yet," he says.

I would have to retrace my path back through the broken up stretch of road and go around the long way. I spend a few minutes searching for the gas station with no luck. Finally I calculate the distance to Kuala Krai and estimate that I should make it. Back I go to the main highway once again. This time I promise myself, no more short cuts—no matter how tempting. I use my spare fuel and make it to K Krai with a small amount to spare. Whew!

From K Krai I continue north to Machang then west to Kuala Nibong near the Thai border. I have finally reached the illusive highway 4 that will take me to Gerik. Highway 4 takes me through Tasik Temenggur Park and across a scenic mountain range to an elevation of 2,527 meters. At 5:00 PM I finally arrive in Gerik, soaked, after riding the last thirty kilometers through pouring rain. My new boots from KL are definitely not waterproof. My feet are slopping wet inside. I have managed to ride an extra 190 *unnecessary* kilometers today, in unbearable heat, and clocked a total of 514 for the day. In spite of it all, I saw some beautiful country and had a good days ride.

In Gerik I search out the Friendly Inn Hotel, recommended by Jen and Marten. I climb a steep flight of stairs to the reception desk and inquire about a room and parking for my bike. The clerk says, "We park your bike in the lobby."

"Where is the lobby?" I inquire.

"Here," replies the clerk, pointing to a space in the room.

"I don't think so," I reply. "It's a big bike." I indicate the size with my hands. "Maybe you better come see." I am thinking it will take several men to haul it up these stairs, *if* the stairwell is wide enough.

The clerk (and I suspect the hotel owner) follows me down the narrow, long staircase and upon seeing my bike exclaims, "*Ohhh, too-oo big!*"

I struggle to contain my laughter. I love how these people display so much expression.

The Friendly Inn clerk quickly comes up with a solution. "We park your bike in my son's store, right here, after closing." He says.

The adjoining shop sells jewelry, tools, appliances big and small, and many other products. It closes at 10:00 PM and I can pull my bike in there before they lock up. Wow, I am honored!

I unpack my bike, do a little laundry and go for dinner before arriving back at the shop a few minutes before 10:00. I hang around while the owner serves the last few customers then pushes some displays to the side and helps me wheel my bike in. I thank him and watch him pull the wrought iron gates across the front of the store and lock them. I can rest easy tonight.

Next morning, after wheeling my bike out of the shop, I have breakfast in the Indian restaurant next door. The waiter is tall, with black hair and very handsome. He is not shy about asking me dozens of questions. Where are you from? Where are you going? Are you married? Where is your husband? Do you have children? How old are you? Aren't you frightened traveling alone? Later, while I pack my bike, a well-dressed Chinese man and his wife stop and talk. I am bombarded with a host of similar questions. As they turn to go the gentleman wishes me a good journey and says, "We will pray for you and for your safety." I am quite touched by their compassion. They simply find it impossible to believe a woman would travel alone in a strange country.

I ride south on highway 76 towards Kuala Kangsar, then turn west and north on highway 1 towards Pulau Pinang. I make a stop at Taiping to visit the zoo and find a charming, clean, little city with tree lined streets, well-kept homes and a picturesque lake surrounded by carefully manicured lawns and gardens. My visit to the zoo is great except that the soles of my shoes come loose again and I am terribly self-conscious about the *clop, clap, clop* on the pavement. Three Indonesian ladies approach me and ask if they can take a picture with me.

"With me?" I repeat, pointing to myself in disbelief.

"Yes," they reply, nodding their heads up and down.

I am certain they did not mistake me for a celebrity with my fancy travelin' clothes and boots with floppin' soles. Later, when I examine the picture I see that the tallest lady comes up to my ears and the other two barely reach my chin—and they are wearing two inch platform sandals. I think they must have thought I was a GIANT!

Clop, clap, clop, clap … I make my way out of the zoo without drawing too much attention to myself; then carry on to Polau Pinang. The rain starts again before I reach P Pinang and crossing the long bridge from the mainland to the island is tense. Traffic is heavy and visibility poor with rain streaming down my visor and windshield. Somehow I find my way into the city of Georgetown and near the area where I should find the Swiss Hotel, which Jen and Marten recommended because of its safe parking. I ride up and down a couple of streets and stop at the SD Motel. It looks fairly decent, like a standard backpacker's lodge, so I check it out.

"Sorry, we're full," says the young gal at the desk.

She kindly gives me directions to the Swiss Hotel. I am just a few blocks away.

I check into the Swiss Hotel with much disappointment. With a name like that you would think it might be fancy. Not so! My room is a small, grey cement walled cubicle with a hard bed and a bathroom consisting of a squat toilet and sink. The shower is down the hall. But for nineteen ringgit, or seven dollars and eighty cents Canadian, how can I complain? On this budget I can travel for a long time.

I unpack my bike, change into dry clothes, and then go for a walk. The rain has stopped and I poke around in some shops before finding an Internet café. Later I stop at the Bamboo Café for dinner. The place is full so I ask a man sitting alone if I can join him. I cannot believe I did that—am I ever getting brave! I wait half an hour for my meal, which is well worth the wait. It is by far the best Nasi Goring (fried rice with chicken) and vegetables I have ever eaten.

This morning I read in the paper that Malaysia aims to be an industrialized country by 2020 (20/20 vision) and that Ireland has chosen Malaysia as its sole overseas regional center to hold the clinical parts of the post-graduate medical examinations.

Next morning I leave my bike parked in the confines of the hotel and walk. I am in search of the Starbucks I remember passing as I rode into the city yesterday. It rained all night and this morning is overcast and muggy. My clothes cling to me. I follow my map to Komtar, a big new shopping centre, and find Starbucks. I order coffee and a muffin and proceed to plan out my day. The coffee is great, but not all Starbucks are equal. The two we frequented in Kuala Lumpur were superb—or was that due to the great company I shared? I am afraid to drink the local coffee. It looks like mud and they lace it with sweetened condensed milk like they do their tea. The thought makes me shudder.

I do an historical walk through the old city stopping at grand old temples and mosques. The Fort on the Esplanade was built in the early eighteen hundreds. There's not much left of it except the crumbling walls and cannons pointing out to sea. Walking back to my hotel, the sky opens up. The rain hit so fast I am immediately soaked to the skin before I can get my umbrella out of my backpack. Might as well put the umbrella back and walk in the rain. In less than ten minutes the rain stops as abruptly as it started.

This evening I try an Indian pizza—Roti with vegetable filling served with traditional curry sauce for dipping. Very good! Sometimes I long for a plain garden salad though, something you seldom get here and when you do it is just not the same as at home.

I need to get out of this city and crappy hotel so I scour the Lonely Planet guide book and decide that tomorrow I will find Miss Loh's Guesthouse in the little village of Teluk Bahang on the west side of the island.

I am in a foul mood when I awake next morning. I hardly slept with the noise of doors opening and closing, people tramping the hallway and stairs, and voices throughout the night. Glad to be moving on, I am packed and gone by 8:30, after waiting for my laundry to return. I fight heavy traffic on my way out of Georgetown en route to the Buddhist Temple *Kek Lo Si*. This is the largest temple in Malaysia. It was started in 1890 and took twenty years to complete. It's gold dome and colorful, rippled, tile roofs edged with lacy looking carvings is an awesome sight.

Kek Lo Si sprawls high on a hillside surrounded by green forests. Approaching from a distance, the first thing I see is the huge bronze statue of the Goddess of Mercy, Kuan Yin. She stands towering on the hill seemingly protecting those around her. A seven-story pagoda reaching thirty meters high is a mixture of Chinese, Thai and Burmese architecture and towers above the main halls. This massive temple consists of many prayer halls, pagodas and bell towers in a stunning setting. It houses gold Buddha statues and life-size monks, thousands of candles and a host of other statues and objects in varying shapes and sizes.

As I climb the long stairs to the old prayer hall I pass beggars sitting or lying in shady spots on the steps with their cups held out. It makes me angry to see all this wealth and still people needing to beg. I wander around the worship halls lined with gold colored Buddhas and colorful statues of oriental women. To enter the new prayer hall I must pay two-ringgit. I am tempted to say to the lady monk, "Be sure you feed those poor people on the steps." I quickly reprimand myself and remember that I am here as a visitor, not to judge.

Leaving the temple I take a gentle winding road through the mountains to Teluk Bahang. I am tired and cranky so once I find Miss Loh's Guesthouse, I check in, park my bike in the garden then take a nap. My room is equivalent to six dollars and thirty cents Canadian—much cleaner, quieter, cheaper, and more pleasant than the Swiss Hotel.

When I awake I go for a walk in the village. Children wave and yell hello as I pass. I return a wave, hello and a smile. I am sure they are used to seeing foreigners here. One young college student from Belgium, who is staying at Miss Loh's, comes here for three months every year.

Teluk Behang is a peaceful little village. I walk to the beach area where the large resort hotels are. They look very classy, but I cannot help but wonder how many of the tourists venture back into the village where the locals live. I imagine they stick to the beaches and shops in the resorts—oh how much they miss.

The sun has gone down when I start my walk back to Miss Loh's. The only light comes from the occasional streetlight positioned between long, dark stretches. I should be frightened but somehow my senses tell me I am safe. I see young and old people still walking in the streets or racing around on their scooters. I see a young man stop and pick up his girlfriend who is waiting in the shadows of the trees. She hops on the back of his motor scooter and away they go. A secret rendezvous! The last street back to the guesthouse is lined with palm trees and poorly lit. I am conscious of my feelings of peace and calm. Logic tells me that I should run this last block, but my heart tells me I am perfectly safe.

In the two short days at Miss Loh's guesthouse I have made friends with some of the other guests and do some sightseeing with them. The temperature has been in the mid to high thirties Celsius. We hike up to some natural pools in the rocks and wade in. The water feels cool initially against the heat of the day, but soon becomes very comfortable and refreshing. We visit the butterfly house and have dinner together. Once again I find myself feeling sad to part, but I know I must. Tomorrow I cross the border into Thailand.

Chapter 8

Thailand, Part I

At 8:30 on the morning of July 4, 2002, I leave Teluk Bahang (Penang) for a scenic ride along the sea to Georgetown. I can't resist a stop at Starbucks for a coffee and croissant before going to the ferry. The crossing takes about fifteen minutes. There is no charge leaving the island—they only charge coming onto the island, either via the bridge or by ferry. I take the expressway to the border at Bt. Kaya Hitam, riding through some rain this morning. The cooler temperature makes it a comfortable ride. By cooler I mean it is no longer 35 degrees Celsius, only 22 to 25.

At the Malaysian border I breeze through customs with my *carnet*. They know exactly what to do. At Thailand customs the procedure is not so easy. Thailand does not recognize the universal carnet; they use their own system called the *white paper*, for vehicles entering their country. However, they insist on stamping my carnet as well. My carnet has to be sent back to Ottawa this month for renewal and I wonder if this will cause a problem since it will not have an exit stamp from Thailand. I guess I will deal with that later. They send me back and forth between buildings several times before finally getting it right and allowing me to cross into Thailand with twenty-eight days on my visa. The border guard points to a little building less than one hundred meters away and says, "You get insurance there." I stop and buy one months motorcycle insurance for less than ten dollars Canadian.

The temperature is extremely hot in Thailand. I ride to Hat Yai before stopping for lunch. As I pull into a large shopping complex, I wonder if my bike will be safe in the open parking lot. I strap my helmet and riding pants to the handle bar, take my jacket and tank bag, and go in search of food. Inside I find a huge food court containing every American franchise imaginable. I pick KFC and go for the chicken wrap—today I cannot face another rice and curry dish. This is Thailand and the Thai people like their food hot. Yes, even my wrap includes some kind of hot sauce. Oh what I would give for a simple salad or plate of mashed potatoes and gravy. The mall is extremely noisy. The main speakers are blasting out loud music, competing with the music and broadcasts coming from individual stores. Combine all that with the constant hum of thousands of people and the noise is *deafening!* I do not linger long at KFC.

I travel a very short distance today. In fact I have only clocked 144 kilometers when I reach Songkhla. I find the Amsterdam Guest House, an older building with clean, comfortable rooms, run by a Dutch couple. The price of my room is two hundred baht per night, or about $7.50 Canadian. I unpack, shower and go for a walk around town.

Songkhla is situated along the edge of the Gulf of Thailand on the east side of the peninsula, and appears to be quieter than some towns I have ridden through. I like it here—I think I will stay a couple of days. After 10:00 PM the owners let me park my bike inside their restaurant, which is attached to the guesthouse. How is that for security!

Next morning, I work on my newsletters and pictures before going to a little Internet café called Dot.Com to update my Web site. I had talked to a young man working there last night and he assured me I could connect my computer. This morning is a different story. The ladies at the desk do not have a clue what I am talking about and the young man from last night is not working this morning. I leave in exasperation and walk up the street stopping at a shop called Technical Solutions. The gal at the desk can speak a little English and she points me back to Dot.Com. I explain to her that they do not understand that I want to connect *my* computer to *their* network. Surree is a tiny lady, very pretty, with long black hair and stands less than 5 feet tall I'm sure. She tells me to come with her. I follow her out of the building and watch her pull out her 100cc scooter. She puts on her helmet and motions for me to get on. I smile and think this is totally irresponsible, but swing my backpack over my shoulder and get on anyway. No helmet for me? Before I can protest we are rolling. We go around the block to Dot.Com and Surree comes in to explain what I want. After a short phone call they show me where I can plug in my computer to their network. Bingo, it works! I gratefully thank Surree and she goes on her way. I am able to work on-line for about two hours for fifty baht (less than two dollars).

I spend two relaxing days in Songkhla—take a walk to the beach, read, write some letters and pack my backup CDs to send home to Carey. I start to read a new book—*Daughter of China*, a true story of love and betrayal, written by Meihong Xu and Larry Engelmann. The book is so good I hate to put it down. In the evening I go to the night market with the Thai waitress, her friend and two other guests. We catch a Tuk-Tuk (pronounced took-took) to the night market. The Tuk-Tuk is a very small pickup truck with benches down both sides of the box that seats ten to twelve people. A canopy covers the top and is just high enough so you do not hit your head when you sit—unless you are taller than I am. The waitress tells the driver where we want to go and we all climb in. When we get out we pay him ten baht each.

The night market is bustling with people. It feels like exhibition week at the fairgrounds. There are hundreds of vendors with everything imaginable to sell, and the aisles are packed with people. There are dozens of food stalls, but the waitress warns us not to try too much unless we have a strong stomach. I avoid the meats and buy some interesting looking sweets. The bustle of the market continues until midnight.

July 7 I decide it is time to get moving. The ride from Songkhla, once I find my way out of town, is most enjoyable. The tropical breezes are blowing strong, but I do not see anyone getting off the highway, so I figure it must be safe to continue. Road signs in the cities are not always easy to read, or to find. I make it to Krabi and try to ask directions to Ao Nang. No one understands me, and tourist information centers are either non-existent or hidden from sight. After about two hours of searching I find the Na Thai Resort, which Jen & Marten had recommended. Gerhardt, the owner, is asking six hundred baht for a cabin. I negotiate with him until we agree on five hundred—less than twenty Canadian. This charming resort has little chalets surrounding a big swimming pool. In high season they rent for nine hundred baht per night. Gerhardt is from Germany and he owns the resort with his Thai lady friend. I spend a couple of nights here and tour the area during the day.

Back in Songkhla I had replied by e-mail to one of the many ads wanting English teachers. When I check my e-mail I have a reply from Lee with TEFL (Teaching English as a Foreign Language). I had asked him if they hire older women. His reply states that women teachers are in high demand here, especially Canadian speaking. He invites me to call him and sit in on a class when I reach Bangkok, or to call on Jim at the school in Thalang, which is on my route.

I ride to the hot pools about fifty kilometers away. The hot mineral water forms in pools created from the roots of trees and rocks. What a perfect natural setting of several little pools with water cascading down keeping the water fresh and over 30°C. I take off my boots and socks, roll up my pant legs and sit with my feet in the hot water for a few minutes. Oh this is so soothing.

Back at the bike a Thai lady comes over to talk to me and tells me about the little island of Ko Lanta, about another 30 kilometers from here. She suggests it is worth spending a day or two there, but I decide to carry on with my original plan. I cannot see everything. Besides, there should always be a reason to come back.

From here I ride to the Crystal Pool via a winding mountainous road, which runs out of pavement for the last four kilometers. I continue and upon arrival follow the walking trail to the Emerald Pools. The hike through the jungle to the emerald pools follows a marshland of clear green water exposing plant life growing on the bottom. The trail is a series of boardwalks built over flood lands. The main pool at the end of the walk is large and a brilliant emerald green. Here I can see where the water bubbles up from underground to form the stream that keeps it flowing. The walk is a photographer's dream and well worth the effort.

I journey back to Na Thai and go for a swim in the pool. The water temperature is quite warm but cools me down from the heat of the day. After dinner Gerhardt invites me to view his pictures of Cambodia and the Angkor Ruins—some great historical places to see. I will try to get there before I continue to India.

July 9 I am on my way to Phuket. My route this morning takes me through mountains of limestone rock shooting up one hundred meters or higher. Some of the cliffs are sheer rock with interesting formations, caves and protrusions resembling stalactites and stalagmites, while others are covered in jungle growth. How can the vegetation possibly grow out of the rock?

I reach Phuket early in the afternoon and stop for lunch and a bank machine. It's extremely hot so I put my big jacket away and dig out my blue jean jacket. The traffic in Phuket is crazy and I have a hard time finding my way to Patong Beach. A man on a little scooter, wearing an orange vest, pulls up beside me and asks where I want to go. I must have really looked lost! Finally I get on the right road and head out into the mountains. The signs are not very precise and once again I find myself going in circles. I know I have to cross that mountain range in front of me, but the signs just do not point in that direction. After taking the same route twice I take a road that looks like it goes across the mountain. Good guess—I wind my way up a steep incline and when I reach the top I can see the ocean. I must be on the right road. Slowly, I make my way down the hill to Patong. I am very hot and tired so I look for a room here. The first place I stop is Patong Beach Bungalows—they want a thousand baht a night (but that includes breakfast—ha-ha)! I ask the clerk if he can direct me to budget accommodations and suddenly he acts as though he cannot understand me. Then a man beside me touches my shoulder and tells me his lady friend knows of a good clean place for three hundred baht. They offer to show me where—all I need to do is follow their little motorbike. I manage to keep them in sight as they weave through the traffic and pull up to the PS2 Motel. True to their word, the room is clean and I can park my bike right outside the door. I talk for a moment with the gentleman before they leave. He is a reporter from Switzerland. He asks, "Are you traveling alone?"

"Yes." I reply.

"Do you have sponsors?"

"No, I didn't try very hard."

"You should have no problem getting sponsors," he says. "What you're doing would make a great story."

I guess I should keep trying but I do not seem to know the right people to contact, and those I have contacted don't seem to think I will succeed.

The roads in Thailand have a sign showing a bicycle and motorbike with words in Thai beneath the pictures. I cannot read them, but it doesn't take me long to figure out that it means motorbikes ride on the shoulder. Now, that would be fine if the shoulders were kept clear of sand, and debris, and parked vehicles, or if the lane did not all of a sudden disappear, or if vehicles did not drive half on the shoulder and half off. And, oh yes, if motorcyclists did not all of a sudden come at you from the wrong direction! No point in arguing though—if an oncoming vehicle pulls out into your lane to pass someone you better just move over to the shoulder and let him pass. There is a definite pecking order on the road—the largest vehicle has the most authority. Motorbikes are down there with bicycles, second to pedestrians who are at the bottom.

I am learning to use the shoulder to my advantage. Whenever I can, I ride near the centre of my lane and move over only for safety sake. When I am stuck behind a line of traffic and cannot get past on the right side, I scoot up the shoulder as far as I can. I know that is not something we would do in Canada, but it does get me past a lot of traffic and out in front where I feel much safer.

July is not tourist season so only a few people occupy Patong Beach. I am told that this beach is packed during the winter months. After breakfast I pack up and head for Katu Beach. Before I get out of Panong I am caught in a downpour—soaked in only a few seconds. I find a place to pull over and run for cover. About ten minutes later it subsides and I am back on the road. The coastline is hilly (mountainous) as I travel towards Karon and Kata Beach. I find the P&T Guesthouse quite by accident and check in. I am staying in places previously referred to me by other bikers. The P&T is run by a Swiss couple named Chuck and Barb. They keep a very clean and attractive establishment. My room is tastefully decorated and comfortable, with a private bathroom and cold running water. I am very satisfied, all this for two hundred baht a night—less than eight dollars Canadian.

I have developed a head cold—from the air conditioning I presume. I have been sneezing and blowing my nose all day today. Barb, the owner of the Guesthouse, kindly sends her maid out to get me some tablets and gives me some of her throat lozenges. What a kind lady! I am finding most people are very kind and helpful.

I walk a few blocks to find a place to eat and browse around momentarily before going back to my room to rest. I will take it easy and get over this head cold before continuing further.

July 11 is a breezy morning. As I eat breakfast in the P&T

Guesthouse garden restaurant, I appreciate the breeze. It is just enough to make this hot temperature comfortable. I must take care of getting my carnet extended—that means sending it back to Canada. A carnet has to be renewed on an annual basis, regardless of how many pages are remaining. Seems a useless task, since all they really need to do is stamp a new expiry date on it. I think I will request that Ottawa fax a letter to the Canadian Embassy in Bangkok authorizing an extension. It seems to me like just another money grab for the government. I must also phone Lee at TEFL today and discuss registering for their course to teach English as a foreign language.

Next morning I feel much better. My head is clear so I am up early and out to find a good Internet café. I find one in Chalong that is cheaper than most and very good. I send off my e-mail to Susan with Canadian Automobile Association (CAA), in regards to my carnet, requesting that they authorize a new expiry date instead of issuing a whole new book. As I prepare to leave it starts pouring rain again, so I stay for a pastry and coffee. Before I am finished the sun is shining. This happens a lot this time of year. I decide to tour around a bit and find a place called Phromthep Cape where a walk up the hill takes me to the lighthouse and sunset viewpoint. I marvel at the beauty and kick myself for leaving my camera at the guesthouse. I follow the coast along a smoothly paved, curvy road around the hills. The view of the ocean takes my breath away!

At one viewpoint I buy fresh pineapple on sticks, ready to eat. Excellent! The first one I pull out of the bag falls off the stick onto the ground and the lady who sold it to me quickly prepares another one. I try to pay her but she refuses any extra money—how kind of her. This is the best pineapple I have ever tasted.

Back at the guesthouse I call Jim Chase with TEFL and set up an appointment for tomorrow at Thalang. He invites me to sit in on a class. Who knows, maybe I will become a teacher. That is just what my parents wanted me to be, many years ago.

Next morning I stop at Thalang and meet with Jim. The meeting is interesting and informative and Jim tells me there is big opportunity to teach English as a foreign language in several countries. I am going to give it some serious thought while I ride on to Bangkok.

I follow the road northeast to Phang-nga bordering the Phang-nga National Park. The day is bright and sunny and the landscape of jagged limestone rock bursting out above the trees is stunning. I arrive in Phang-nga early—there is just so much to see that my riding time is cut short. I decide to ride out to Phang-nga Bay before looking for a room. As I approach the bay all the tour boat vendors are waving me down. They all want to nab any tourists that come at this time of year. Their prices range from three hundred to eight hundred baht. I find one that is leaving in five minutes and barter the price down to two hundred and fifty. I am ushered onto a large, canvas covered, long tail boat with a large Thai group. I cannot understand a thing the tour guide is saying and the boat is over crowded so I quickly get a seat and make sure I keep it for the duration of the tour. The islands are fascinating—we cruise through the waters to Kotapu and Kaopingkan (James Bond Island), through Knaotapu and Tham Lod Caves and stop at Kohpanyee, a floating Muslim Fishing Village.

When we dock at the floating village, the Thai tourists walk straight for the market. Not me, I stroll on boardwalks running through the village to see how these people live. Most houses are built adjoining the main walkways and some a meter away connected by small wooden bridges. Children are playing on the sidewalks and stop to look at me as I pass. I discover a large cement pad, fenced for a recreation area, where children are playing basketball and kicking a soccer ball around. Around another corner I see several young boys playing—they are jumping or falling off posts that line the sidewalk, landing on their backs in the water. What fun! I am tempted to join them. I make my way back to the shops with enough time for a quick browse through the market before returning to the boat. This has been a great adventure, even though I could not understand the tour guide and my companions. They were very kind to me. They laughed and smiled a lot and I am sure talked about this crazy lady who joined them and is traveling all by herself.

Back at the Guest House I relax on the covered patio and catch up on my journal writing. It rains hard most of the afternoon. I watch a man ride by on his motorcycle using one hand to hold an umbrella over his head. He is wearing shorts, shirt, flip-flops on his feet and no helmet! I get caught at an Internet café during one of these downpours and a very pleasant lady lends me her umbrella. I try to protest but she insists, telling me she has another one and can pick this one up at the guesthouse later.

July 15 I continue north towards Bangkok. I will try to make a few more miles today. There is so much to see, but this is day eleven on my

143

twenty-eight-day visa. I ride northeast on highway 415, then north on 41, which eventually becomes 4 after Chumphon.

At Chumphon I stop at a restaurant for lunch and two men in a pickup truck pull up behind me. Neither of them attempts to speak to me, they just peer closely at my bike. One of the men is talking on his cell phone and I get a very uncomfortable feeling as they drive away. Shortly after I enter the restaurant two police officers ride up on their motorbikes. They do not come into the restaurant; they just take a good look at my bike and leave. I do not like the feelings I'm getting so I quickly eat and leave. My mind flashes back to my friend Geoff, from home. His words were "Listen to your instincts, Doris. Women are very intuitive; don't brush your feelings off." I never did see them again and have no idea what that was all about. I continue north up this narrow peninsula to Prachuap Khiri Khan before stopping for the day. I have put on 485 kilometers today, which is plenty in this heat. I will have a short ride to Bangkok tomorrow.

By 8:00 o'clock next morning I am riding through beachside resorts and am surprised that no one speaks English in this area. My guess is these resorts are not as popular with foreigners. Before reaching Phetchaburi I am stopped by a police roadblock checking motorists going both directions. I feel a knot in my stomach as I approach, but they wave me through. Upon reaching Phetchaburi I encounter another roadblock. The officer asks where I am going. I reply "Bangkok." He waves me through without asking for any paperwork. Finally I reach Bangkok. The traffic is horrendous! I follow the directions given to me by Marten and Jen and, after some trial and error, find the Bamboo Guesthouse in the center of the city. I park my bike near the right wall of the lobby next to two motorbikes with German license plates. My bike will be safe here. The Bamboo Guesthouse is secured with a steel fence and gates that are kept locked at all times.

I get a room for one hundred and seventy-five baht, and unpack my bike before going for a walk. I am attracted to signs in just about every store window—*English teachers wanted, French teachers wanted*. I cannot help but feel that these are a message for me to look further. I stop at one such sign and go in to inquire. They invite me to sit in on a class. The teacher is an American and he is tutoring three college students. After an hour I am thinking, *what a joke. These poor students are wasting their money. I could do better than that and I don't have training*—how pathetic.

As I walk back to the guesthouse I notice that police officers wear white facemasks, like a doctor's mask, for some protection against the pollution. Standing at a controlled intersection waiting for the walk light to change, I watch people walk every which way ignoring the lights. Beside me, on a very tall stool, sits a petite, good-looking police officer wearing his white mask and white gloves resting his ticket pad on his lap. I am curious, so I stand there for a couple of light changes to see if he writes anyone a ticket. People are jay walking everywhere—the officer remains on his post. I am not sure what he is looking for—maybe nothing, maybe just putting in his shift.

Next morning I call Lee with TEFL and pay him a visit. I enroll in the TEFL course for twenty-two thousand baht. This will give me a certificate to teach English as a foreign language. Lee refers me to Jennifer, the head teacher for one of the NAVA (private) English schools. I get lost trying to find her school so call and make an appointment for tomorrow. Traffic is terrible and it takes me an hour to get back to the guesthouse just twelve kilometers away.

Early the next morning I leave the guesthouse for my appointment with Jennifer. My first mistake of the day is taking my motorbike instead of the public transit system. I miss my turn onto Phahon Yothin Road and have to find a place to turn around. I come back to the lights and see a green arrow pointing straight through and to the left, but nothing right. I really need to go right and do not see any sign saying no right turn, so I patiently wait out the traffic and turn right—right into a little traffic cop waiting for me. He waves his arms for me to stop, takes off his white mask and asks for my license.

"You no turn right here," he says.

Remember I am driving on the left in Thailand. "The sign says no U-turn, it doesn't say no right turn," I exclaim.

He argues with me and I repeat my claim. Finally he says, "I have to give you ticket, is that okay?"

"No," I reply. "The sign doesn't say *No right turn!*"

We argue back and forth a few minutes more, then he says, "You come to police station with me, okay?"

"I have an appointment at 9 o'clock," I reply. "I am already late."

Once again he asks, "I write you a ticket, okay? You pay ticket."

Finally it dawns on me, he wants money! "How much?" I ask.

"Four hundred baht," he replies.

"I don't have four hundred baht on me."

"How much?" he asks.

"One hundred baht," I reply.

He laughs and says, "I write you a ticket, okay?"

"No it's not okay," I repeat indignantly. "But you do what you have to do."

The officer writes a ticket and hands it to me. I put out my hand for my license and he says, "You get this back when you come to police station and pay ticket."

"I need my license to drive. You will give me another ticket if I drive without it," I protest, feeling my anger rise. I reach up and put my thumb on my license. With a couple of tugs it comes free and I quickly tuck it and the ticket into my tank bag and snap the lock closed. The officer turns on his heel, gets on his motorbike and rides away.

Wow, I am free—a little shaken, but free! I continue on to my appointment thinking maybe I don't want to stay in Thailand after all.

I reach the Nava office and apologize to Jennifer for being a half hour late.

"Don't worry about it," she replies with a smile. "In Thailand any time within the hour is still on time." Jennifer is from New Zealand and has been managing one of three Nava English speaking schools for Khun Tairak for two years. She is about forty-five years old, five foot eight inches tall, with sandy-brown hair and a sturdy frame. She has a wonderful personality and a strong New Zealand accent. I immediately connect with her. She shows me around the school and explains that 'Khun' is a term of respect, as 'Mr.' is in our language.

Khun Tairak arrives shortly. He is tall and slim, has beautiful black hair that all Thais are blessed with, and very good-looking. I later discover his heritage is Chinese Thai, thus the height—native Thais are very short. Khun Tairak takes me across town to one of his other schools. He is a very aggressive driver and I find myself watching attentively at his fast and seemingly dangerous maneuvers. He speaks very good English and explains that his schools are mainly geared to students who want to take extra English classes in addition to what they are taught in the regular school system. These are the families that can afford to spend the money on extra classes for English, math, science, computers and music. Many children go to classes six and seven days a week. By the end of our meeting he offers me a job teaching ten to twelve year olds conversational English four hours a day for the next eight Saturdays. The pay is three hundred and fifty baht per hour.

"But I don't have my certificate yet, I am just starting the TEFL course." I explain.

"That's okay," he replies. "You speak good English. Canadians are the best teachers because they speak very clearly. We are short of teachers and I think you can do the job."

I am honored at his confidence in me and decide to take his offer.

Later I stop at the TEFL office and talk to Lee. He offers me twenty hours a week, Monday through Friday, at a school about twenty minutes from here. I cannot believe this! I guess I will be staying in Bangkok for a few weeks. Next job is to look for an apartment. Lee gives me a couple of addresses to check out—apartments where other English speaking teachers live. I find a little one-room apartment with a bathroom, furnished with a large bed, including a very hard mattress, nightstand, small round table and two chairs, small fridge and wardrobe closet. The bathroom is about one meter square with a western style toilet, sink, showerhead and floor drain. When you shower the water covers the whole bathroom. The walls are cement and in bad need of paint. The total area of the apartment is 3.9 X 5.6 meters. The rent is twenty-six hundred baht a month, or about ninety-seven dollars Canadian. I think I will take it.

The next few days I spend at the markets shopping for items to decorate my apartment. No need for blankets in this heat so I find a colorful set of sheets, pillows, towels, small floor mats, candles, toaster, teakettle, two plates, two cups, two glasses and two sets of utensils—two of everything, just in case I have company. Then I go in search of paint to paint the walls before I move in.

Saturday I am up early and at my new apartment to clean and paint. Oh yes, it has been cleaned by the cleaning staff but not to my liking. Anyway, it is just one room; I can have that painted and the floor scrubbed in no time. The cleaning lady stops by when I am about half finished painting. She does not speak much English, but enough to say, "You need man."

"No," I reply, "Too much trouble."

I can hear her laughing as she continues down the hall.

I finish my work early enough to go shopping with Caryn, a lady from Winnipeg, also teaching and living here. I start my TEFL course tomorrow and teach my first class on Monday. I need some dress clothes. A skirt, a couple of blouses and a pair of shoes is all I need. It amazes me how little I can get by on.

After my second day of teaching I am exhausted. Tuesday evening I am in bed early and sound asleep when the ringing of the telephone startles me. I look at my watch, 11:00 PM. *Who could be calling me at this hour?* I answer "Hello" in a groggy voice. It's May, a Chinese-Thai lady Caryn and I met yesterday, also living in this apartment. "Are you lonely?" she asks.

Oh my God, what is this! Is this lady is trying to pick me up?

"No," I snap. "I'm tired and have to work tomorrow." That was a lie. Tomorrow is a Buddhist holiday and no one works on Buddhist holidays.

July 24, I am not sure what they call this holiday but it falls on the full moon and the tradition is to walk around the temple three times for good luck throughout the year. I go to the temple with the intention of walking around it three times but when I arrive I think, what if I walk the wrong direction, will that bring me bad luck, or worse yet—offend someone? In the end I leave without doing the walk and go shopping instead.

Finding clothes large enough for me is not an easy task. I am not a big person but the Thai women are *tiny*. I finally find a black skirt and one blouse that fit. I guess I will have to get clothes made if I decide to stay awhile.

Later that evening around 8:30, as I am walking home from an Internet café, I see a man riding an elephant down the street. How odd, in the middle of busy city traffic. It looks awfully strange to me but no one else seems to pay any attention.

After the third day of teaching my Monday to Friday classes, Miss Sally, the assistant manager of Udom Suksa School, calls me. She wants to discuss a full time contract. Do I want to commit to that right now? I still have half the world to travel around. The plus side of signing a full time contract is that the school applies and pays for your working visa and entrance visa. My entrance visa expires in a few days and I will have to leave the country and re-enter Thailand to obtain another one. I wonder if, by accepting her offer, my dream of riding around the world would fall by the way side … I turn down her offer.

To get back and forth to my TEFL class on Sundays I catch a tuk-tuk. This is a smaller version of the one I experienced in Songkhla. It holds six people in the back and one more person in the front seat next to the driver. For Thai people, this is a lot of room but when you put a couple of 'ferangs' (the Thai term for foreigners) in the back, it gets crowded. The seats are low and, for us taller people, our knees end up close to our chest. The drivers are crazy as they weave in and out of traffic. I make sure I hang on and try not to slide onto the person next to me. If I sit right at the back by the entrance I am especially careful to hold on—one could easily slide right out the open doorway. When it rains the driver stops and lowers heavy plastic curtains (attached to the exterior of the box) to cover the open windows. There is no cover for the door so if you are sitting next to the doorway you may still get wet. One day the driver pulls into a gas station and fuels up with all seven passengers still aboard. I cannot believe it! That would be a definite offense at home. None-the-less, it is easier to take a tuk-tuk than ride my bike in these jam-packed streets.

I am amazed at the local motorcyclists on their small bikes. They wear no protective clothing, flip-flops or sandals on their feet and usually no helmets. Added to this, they pack four or five people on this little machine. It gives a whole new meaning to "family transportation".

There are numerous big shopping Plazas throughout Bangkok and I do not have to go far to find good stores, movie theatres, electronic shops and anything else my heart desires.

My Thai visa expires on August 1 so I begin to make plans to ride to Cambodia for a week. I will have to fit this in between weekend classes and see as much of Cambodia as time permits.

Chapter 9

Cambodia—Border Run

Wednesday, July 31, I make my border run to Cambodia. I leave early and painstakingly fight my way out of Bangkok traffic to highway 305 heading northeast. At Nakhon Nayok I go east on highway 33 to Aranyaprathet, Thailand and the Cambodia border. The countryside becomes flat as I ride farther east. I pass acres of rice paddies covered in water and off in the distance people working—in water that must surely come to their knees.

Finally I reach the border, and before I am even close to stopping, I am flanked by runners offering to help me through Customs. One little man directs me to the Thai window and offers to watch my bike. Although apprehensive, I do not want to carry all my stuff, so I make sure my tank bag is locked, tie my helmet onto the handle bar and throw jacket over it all. I take my visa and *white paper* to the window and patiently wait in line. There are several other foreigners here, probably doing the same as me—renewing their Thai visa. It takes the customs officers a few minutes to process the white paper for the bike but eventually they return with my copy and my visa, both stamped with an exit stamp from Thailand. I return to the bike and my little guard directs me across the road to the Cambodia office. The line here is short and in no time I have a Cambodian visa pasted into my passport, claiming one whole page. I hand the clerk my Thai white paper for the bike, but he shows no interest so I stuff it in my pocket and leave.

Back at the bike I pay my guard one hundred baht. He accepts it graciously but in seconds, turns and asks for two hundred baht. I am becoming familiar with the value of the baht and how local people think all foreigners are rich. They try hard to squeeze more money from us, but this time I refuse to give him more. He makes a few grumbling sounds but does not persist, so I reckon I have given him enough.

I don my helmet, jacket and gloves and ride through a huge cement arch crowned with three steeples, flanked with a smaller arch on either side, with a shield and statue of a lion at the top. The signage on the top says 'Kingdom of Cambodia'.

Immediately across the border is a tall monument standing in the middle of a traffic circle edged with a cement curb and surrounded by a very wide dirt road. Around the outer edges of the traffic circle are vendor stalls, a half dozen well-kept buildings, parked trucks, busses, tuk-tuks, bicycles, 100cc motorbikes, rickshaws, two wheeled wooden carts with side racks loaded down with produce, and hundreds of people. Garbage is strewn everywhere. Children approach the ferangs with their hands folded in the prayer position at their chest, looking up at their victim with those huge dark eyes, asking for money.

The first thing I notice is that traffic here is driving on the right side of the road. I make a mental note to keep that in mind as I maneuver through the chaotic circle. *Surely it will be better once I am away from the border gates.* I escape the traffic circle only to be faced with a road of rocks embedded into the dirt. The road from edge to edge is rocks of every shape and size—big, small, round, square, smooth, sharp—with the exception of one track about thirty centimeters wide. It appears the rocks have been pushed aside or picked off and everyone attempts to occupy this path. I'm thinking, maybe it's just for bikes—but soon realize *not!* Even the vehicles jostle to keep one wheel in the track. As I said before, the pecking order goes by size and I fall way down near the bottom of the chain. I can only hope the road improves once I am out of this border town. The rock surface continues like this for a treacherous ten kilometers. I seize the track whenever possible then carefully move back onto the bed of rocks when a larger vehicle approaches. Other bikers had warned me about the roads in Cambodia, but never in my wildest imagination did I anticipate this!

Finally I reach the end of the rocks only to be faced with a dirt road full of potholes so big I know if I hit one I would probably damage my bike. I encounter a couple of wooden bridges wide enough for one truck. The deck is constructed of wood planks and covered with a thick layer of hard packed dirt. In places the dirt has worn away exposing the planks and leaving a drop of seven or eight centimeters on either side.

I pass rice fields and yards with little shacks built of wood and straw standing on meter high stilts. Children run naked playing in the grass and trees. My first thought is, how sad. As quickly as that thought comes it passes as I recall my years growing up on the farm. In the summer months, on those very hot days, we dressed in only our panties in our pre-school years. We were happy—these children are too.

After fifty kilometers and two hours of riding I reach Sisiphon and look for a motel. I have only ridden 456 kilometers from Bangkok but it has been an exhausting day. I check into my room before taking a short ride out of town to inspect the road for tomorrow. I would really like to visit the Angkor Ruins in Siam Reap, which are within two hundred kilometers of here. I ride for about two kilometers and turn back, deciding that I do not want to tackle these roads alone. Recent rains have left the road full of mud and water holes, potholes and ruts. I think I will give it a miss for now.

I ride back to the motel and park my bike before going for a walk in the streets of Sisiphon. School age children carrying trays and bowls on their heads yell out hello. I respond with a wave and hello and they come over to talk to me. These children are studying English in school and are anxious to practice on a foreigner. They follow me as I walk and are full of questions. The streets are dusty and littered with garbage. I pass by a market busy with people buying and selling. I meet another lady carrying a large bowl, filled with melons, on her head. That is quite a talent—I wish I could do that.

I have a wonderful sleep without the constant noise of the city. The noise never stops in Bangkok—the constant drone of traffic, people, music, chanting and the ringing of bells from the temples *never* stops! Here, in Sisiphon, it has been a quiet night and I actually slept in. At 8:00 AM I am packing up to go, but decide to check my bike chain first. I discover it is loose, so I pull out my tools and proceed to tighten it. In minutes I have an audience, including the cleaning lady standing in the doorway of a room she is cleaning. I finish the job then walk over to the cleaning lady and, in a game of charades, ask if I can use her cleaning cloth to wipe my hands. She gives me a cloth and squirts soap on my hands, then motions me towards the sink. I rinse my hands and she is right there to squirt more soap on them, then hands me a dry towel. I feel so grateful! It seems like such a small gesture but means so much when you are in a strange country far from home.

My audience watches me ride away. The town is bustling with activity. I pass 100cc motorbikes pulling hand made, two wheeled, wooden trailers loaded down with produce. I come upon one young motorcyclist pulling a trailer complete with wooden side racks, just big enough to hold a big old sow. I am sure this rig is on its way to market. I stop a couple of blocks ahead and get my camera out so I can take a picture when he goes by. When I turn, with my camera ready, he is nowhere to be seen. Just my luck! He must have turned off on a side street and I do not get the photo—but this is one picture I will keep in my memory forever.

I appreciate the bad road knowing I still have to cross ten kilometers of rock I just came through yesterday. I arrive at the border without incident, get my exit stamp for Cambodia and walk across the road to Thailand. This is a small border crossing so I find myself at the same wicket I was at less than 24 hours ago. The clerk stamps my passport giving me another thirty days in Thailand, then stamps my photo-copied white paper for the bike. I ask, "Don't you need to make a new white paper for my bike?"

"No, all finished." he replies.

"Can I drive in Thailand with this?" I inquire.

"Yes, no problem, this paper good." he states.

I am almost positive they should be filling out a new form, but he dismisses me with a wave. I return to my bike hoping this does not present a problem later.

A few kilometers down the road, a patrol officer on a motorcycle stops me and asks to see my carnet. My thoughts go wild thinking I am in trouble because of the photo copied white paper. I have learned to keep my documents handy so I unlock my tank bag, pull out my papers and hand them to the officer. He studies the paper (I can tell he does not understand anything on it), folds it back up, hands it to me and waves me on with a smile. Oh, why do I feel this will be trouble later!

My ride back to Bangkok is uneventful. I breath deeply of the fresh air knowing the pollution I face once back in the city. Already I am wondering where I will make my next border run when these thirty days expire.

Chapter 10

Thailand, Part II

I get lost coming back into Bangkok and somehow find myself on the wrong side of the airport. I use major landmarks to get my general direction. The traffic is so horrendous one has to be extra cautious, which makes looking for street signs difficult. I finally reach an area that looks familiar and soon find myself in the Pohan Yotin area where I live. I am proud of myself for having found my way in and out of this crazy city.

Teaching hours do not take up my whole day, so I have plenty of time to see the sights, read, update my Web site and keep up with e-mails. I try different restaurants—eating out is very cheap, unless of course one frequents restaurants that serve western style food. Today I try the famous Thai soup, *Tom Yum*, which I am told is a favorite Thai dish. It is packed full of jumbo shrimp, mushrooms, vegetables and chili peppers in a coconut milk broth. The waitress sets the soup in front of me. "This looks excellent." I comment. She smiles her appreciation and returns to the kitchen.

I take my soupspoon and swallow the hot broth. Immediately I start to cough, choke and sputter. My nose starts to run and I break out in a sweat. I wipe my brow, blow my nose and try to compose myself. *Okay, let's try this again*, I think to myself. I gingerly take another sip and the coughing and choking grasps me once more. Wow, those chili peppers are hot. Once again I compose myself and sneak a peak towards the kitchen to see if anyone is witnessing this spectacle. The cook and waitress must be giggling behind the kitchen door. No one told me about the hot chili peppers. I am determined to eat this, so I very slowly take the broth and a shrimp in my mouth and hold it there for a few seconds. Ah, this is the trick. I can actually prepare my palate for the heat of the hot chili peppers. By the time I finish the bowl I am enjoying Tom Yum. When I leave the restaurant a blast of 38°C humid air hits me. The sweat immediately returns to my brow and my mind draws a comical comparison to the effects of the soup and the weather.

Finding a good haircut for a woman who wears her hair short is a challenge. Hairdressers are used to working with long, thick hair, not short and fine hair like mine. I stop in at a shop that looks clean and not too busy. My first problem is that no one understands English. There are three hairdressers and not one understands me. I should probably leave, but they are not about to let me go. A petite, young lady with beautiful long black hair leads me to a shampoo chair and I reluctantly sit down. She reclines the chair and I lay my head back into the sink. This chair is heaven—no hard rim around my neck. Joi begins the meticulous job of shampooing my hair. Shampoo, rinse, shampoo, rinse … like a ritual she performs the task for about ten minutes. I could fall asleep and I am thinking, Oh, please don't stop, I don't care what the cut is like; the scalp massage is worth whatever the outcome. The cost for this wonderful treatment is less than six dollars Canadian.

Monday morning I get a call from Ling, at Text and Talk. She asks me to tutor an elderly gentleman, a retired judge who would like some conversational time to practice and improve on his already adequate English. I wonder if I am qualified to handle this but Ling assures me I will do fine. "He really just wants conversation," she states.

August 7 is my first class with Khun Pon. I am a bit nervous—after all, he is a judge. Is he going to find out I am working illegally and have me deported? Or thrown in jail? Once I meet my student I soon relax. I let him choose the topics of discussion today and of course he starts out asking questions about Canada then gradually throws in a few personal questions like "where is your husband, do you have children, where are they?" et cetera. I tell him about my motorcycle trip around the world. He is fascinated and at the same time shocked that I dare to travel alone.

"What does your family think about you traveling alone?" he asks with much concern.

I assure him that they are okay with it and very supportive. Over the next weeks of classes with Khun Pon I learn as much from him as he does from me. Some days I choose the topics and ask about their health care, their government, what they are doing about their pollution problem … the pay for this class is very minimal but the rewards are immeasurable.

On August 10 Caryn and I take a bus to Kau San Road in Banglampu area. Kau San Road is a popular tourist area where most backpackers stay. The streets are packed with neat restaurants, gift shops, clothing shops, massage parlors, tattoo parlors, and crowded with thousands of people. We sit for awhile in a sidewalk café watching the bustle of activity before we split and go our separate ways. Caryn has already done the touristy things down here so she is going to meet a friend. I decide to hire a tuk-tuk to take me around to see the sights. These sight seeing tuk-tuks are like a large tricycle with a covered back seat for two and a single seat up front for the driver. I explain to the driver, Poi, what places I want to see and he gives me a price of twenty baht. For this price he would take me to five attractions—sounds like a great deal to me. Our first stop is Wat Pari Nayok which houses some very large Buddhas; then we stop at a Thai fashion store—a garment factory where suits, dresses, and other clothing are custom made. As soon as I walk in I wonder why Poi brought me here. I look around briefly and return to the tuk-tuk where I find Poi lying in the back seat drinking from a little brown bottle. He is surprised to see me and says, "Energy drink, energy drink …" I am thinking, right, how dumb do you think I am?

Poi takes his place in the driver's seat and explains the *promotion deal* to me. If I stay fifteen minutes in the store he will receive a fuel voucher.

"I hired you to take me sightseeing, not shopping," I exclaim rather sharply.

"We go see another Wat then I take you to the Gem Factory. You will like it there; they sell emeralds, rubies, and diamonds—lots of precious stones. You only stay fifteen minutes and I get fuel voucher."

I find myself softening and think to myself, what the heck, I guess I can browse in a gem gallery for fifteen minutes. "Okay, but after that you take me to the places I have asked to see."

Poi agrees, seems like we have come to an understanding.

We continue on to the next Wat, which I realize later was not even on the route I requested. When Poi stops the tuk-tuk he turns to talk to me and nonchalantly brushes his hand across my knee. I abruptly pull my backpack onto my lap and get out. I am feeling some bad vibes here.

As I walk up the path to the Wat I notice a man in front of me. I follow him into the Wat where he sits cross-legged in the prayer chamber. I stand for a moment wondering if I should be here. Just as I am about to turn and leave he looks up and invites me to sit. We sit silently for a minute before he starts asking me all kinds of personal questions. Then he tells me about an exporter who sells rubies and emeralds for one thousand US dollars that I could sell in America for two thousand. This man claims to be a customs agent and says, "Thai students do this all the time to pay for their education."

I let him talk a moment longer before getting up to leave. I go directly to the tuk-tuk, pay Poi his twenty baht and tell him I am walking. He displays shock and surprise and wants to know why. I say, "I have had enough of this scam, I am walking." and quickly turn and walk away. Feeling a little nervous, I watch anxiously all around me until I am back on a busy sidewalk where I feel safe and can continue sightseeing. As I make my way back to Kau San Road I realize Poi had driven past several of the spots I wanted to see and did not even point them out to me. What kind of a tour guide was he, or what were his ulterior motives?

Once back at Kau San Road I decide to go for a Thai massage before meeting up with Caryn. I pass by several shops before stepping into one that looks quite busy—*must be good*, I think to myself. They are able to fit me in so I take a seat and wait for ten minutes before being ushered into a large back room lined with single beds built with sturdy wood frames, running the length of the room. Must be ten beds placed side by side with enough room at the foot of them to create a walkway. First thing I notice is a man on one of the beds getting worked on. This is obviously co-ed and I am relieved to see we keep our clothes on for a Thai massage. Mae, my massage therapist who is a tiny little lady, probably no more than four feet ten inches tall, instructs me to lie on my back and relax. She gets on the foot of the bed and begins to work on my legs. Oh, that feels so good. I hear the man a couple of beds down making an occasional moan and ouch sound. What's wrong with him, I think. Then Mae places her arm at the top of my leg where it joins the hip and leans all her weight on me. I gasp and almost hit the roof! That is a sensitive area. But the treatment is just beginning. This little lady might be small but she is certainly powerful. She sits on my legs as she works farther up my body and uses her whole body weight to work out tense muscles. Just when I start to relax and enjoy this she hits another sensitive spot extracting a gasp from me. Then she sits at the head of the bed with her back against the wall and knees bent to her chest. She instructs me to sit in front of her with my back at her knees. She commences to pull my body backwards over her knees, bending, pulling and twisting me into positions I did not know were possible. I'm glad I've been practicing my yoga on a regular basis or she might injure me! I am beginning to understand the noises from the gentleman down the line and wonder if I can take an hour of this treatment. I manage to hang in there and vow never to do that again. That was torture, not a massage—but maybe a person could become accustomed to it if experienced on a regular basis. Definitely something everyone should try at least once.

There are many Buddhist holidays in Thailand. Today, August 12, is the Queen's birthday—warranting a holiday complete with a Royal Parade. Her Majesty Queen Sirikit was born in 1932. She is as highly respected as the King and considered the mother to all people. Khun Pon told me that the Thai people have tremendous respect for their King and Queen. "You will never hear anything bad said about our King and Queen," he said. "They have done a lot for our people."

My weekend English classes are wonderful but if I am going to stay here for awhile I need to get more work, so I start checking out other short term jobs posted on the Internet and at the Nava schools. I am surprised and happy to get several replies for interviews, along with a couple of offers. They are so short of "English-speaking" teachers here that jobs are plentiful. I will think about these and make a decision later this month.

Train Ride to Malaysia

At the end of August my visa expires so I plan a train ride to Penang, Malaysia. I have never traveled by train before and suppose this will be a good opportunity. I purchase a return ticket for about seventy-five dollars Canadian and board at Bang Sue train station at 14:10 on August 25. My arrival time in Penang is 12:55 PM August 26. The train is long and I am booked into car number four. The seats are like those on a school bus, except they are harder with much higher backs. I am thankful to find a pillow on my seat, which I use to place between my head and the window. The train is noisy and it sways from side to side. The image I had in my head was one of a smooth steady ride—not this train. At 6:30 PM the steward makes his way up the aisle transforming the bench seats into beds. I am grateful for the opportunity to lie down and rest my aching back.

Sometime later I am nudged awake, by what I am not sure. The train is stopped. Maybe it was the lack of motion that awakened me. I look at my watch; it reads 6:30 AM. I convert my bed back to the bench seat then look out the window to see if there is a sign on the train station. My eyes scan over the people mulling around on the platform—people carrying trays and baskets of food to sell to the passengers. I spot the sign 'Hat Yai'. According to my map the next stop should be the Malaysian border. I am hungry but the hawker's food does not interest me, so I settle for my fruit and buy a coffee. Another ten minutes pass before the train starts to move again and in an hour we reach the border crossing at Padang Basar. This is a different crossing from the one I rode across two months earlier. All the passengers file into the Thailand customs line to get stamped out of the country then file into another line to be stamped into Malaysia. There is no charge for a visa stamp in my passport upon entering Malaysia. I am given thirty days—irrelevant since I will only be here four days, just long enough to apply for and receive a ninety-day visa back into Thailand. All goes very smoothly at the border. The crossing is so much easier without my bike.

At about 1:00 PM the train reaches Butterworth, Malaysia. I've spent almost twenty-four hours on this very slow moving train. I find my way to the ferry terminal and for sixty cents cross the strait to Georgetown. I feel like an old hand at this, having been here two months ago. In Georgetown I catch a taxi to the Thai consulate only to find that the office is near closing and all I can do is pick up the application forms to fill out and bring back tomorrow—which I do along with two photos, my passport and thirty-three ringgit.

August 28, I pick up my passport and immediately check the

length of stay they've given me. My passport is stamped for sixty days and I question the clerk stating that I applied for ninety days. He informs me that I must go to the Thai Consulate in Bangkok and pay five hundred baht to get the remaining thirty days authorized.

August 29 I board the train once again and prepare for the painfully slow ride back to Bangkok. The border crossing goes smoothly again and I cannot help but wish it were that easy with my bike. I arrive back in Bangkok around 11:00 on the morning of August 30. There is a one-hour time change and today it works to my advantage. Once I go to the Thai consulate I will be set for three months before I have to do this again.

I am feeling homesick. My teaching schedule is not keeping me busy enough with classes and I am having doubts about my decision to stay in Bangkok. It is not the greatest place in Thailand to be with all the pollution and ten million people. They say the population is seven million but you can add another three million foreigners to that count. I send an e-mail to my sisters saying, "So, who is spending Christmas in Thailand this year?" Thoughts are powerful and I believe whatever you put out there will come back to you.

Classes are winding down and mid September brings exams for my weekend students. I admire these young children. Most are enthusiastic about improving their English and weekend classes are just part of life. About this same time one of the Nava schools offer me two contracts; one is a full time position requiring a one-year commitment and the other is a fifteen-week contract teaching four adult classes for an electronics department of government employees. The adult classes will start on October 1, four hours a day, and pays five hundred baht per hour. Wow ... I know I do not want to make a one-year commitment but I am not sure I have the ability or confidence to teach adults. I meet with Khun Peng and Susan, who own the Nang Wang Nava branch, and discuss my concerns. By the end of the meeting they have convinced me I can handle the job. I can also continue my weekend classes.

My new job is near the Victory Monument; about an hour by bus and sky train from my apartment. The hours of the classes are scheduled for 7:00 to 9:00 AM and 4:30 to 6:30 PM, to accommodate the employees work schedule. I decide to look for an apartment near there to avoid the wasted travel time four times a day. I find one overlooking the Peace Park with a great view and a much bigger room. I can arrange the furniture to make it look like two rooms. I talk the management into painting the walls before I move in. My bed has a square wood bookshelf headboard about a meter high that I position in the middle of the room beside the wall, utilizing the headboard as a room divider. I move the huge wardrobe closet across from the bed leaving a path about a meter wide between the two. The bathroom door exits at the foot of the bed and another door to a small patio. The other end of the room, where the entrance is, contains two armchairs, a coffee table, fridge, and small wall shelf with a mirror—a cozy little sitting room. Wow, this is luxury! I almost feel guilty when I think of the families of four who live in tiny apartments like the one I leave behind. We are such a spoiled society!

If I am going to be teaching working class adults I need a couple of suits; so I find a tailor and order an outfit consisting of pants, skirt, jacket and two blouses. I also have them alter the pants I bought when I first arrived. Seems I have lost weight in the past month. Must be the heat; I cannot walk out the door without breaking out in a full body sweat.

October 1 is my first day of corporate classes. I decide to take my motorbike and end up on the wrong road heading towards a tollbooth entrance. There is a patrol officer monitoring traffic and I explain my mistake to him expecting to get a lashing and ticket, but he kindly stops traffic so I can cross the freeway and make a U-turn. After a few more mistakes I finally make it to class with ten minutes to spare. My class goes very well—students range from twenty to forty-five years in age and are keen on learning. The government is paying for their classes so they must get a good report. Teachers are held in high respect and it shows in each of them.

I continue to ride my bike to and from work and after a few days it hits me—this is like a driving arcade game. One of those machines you sit at and try to avoid the obstacles. I start out cautiously; swerve to avoid that little scooter, change lanes—look out for the taxi driver! Swerve into the curb lane—whoa, watch that bus, he's bigger than you, get out of the curb lane, oh-oh, there's a police officer, they don't like bikers, look out for the traffic circle ahead—all the vehicles crowd into the circle and squeeze their way out the sides. Look out behind you! That scooter's trying to squeeze into a thirty-centimeter space and a dozen little motorbikes are closing in on you. I squeeze up between the lines of traffic and stop with one hundred other bikes at a red light! When I finally arrive home for the day I breathe a sigh of relief, wipe my brow and smile. "I'VE WON! I can go do it all over again tomorrow."

In my free time I walk to Siam Square or a street market, taking in the activity around me. I pass men on street corners playing checkers with bottle caps on a hand made board. They are having great fun.

I walk past beggars, some lying on the ground, some sitting or standing. The tourist books tell you not to contribute to the begging, but I watch the local people drop coins into the hat or cup as they pass. Thai people are very generous. I am told begging has become an organized business, run by pimps. The most shocking incident I witness is a baby no more than a year old, sitting on an overhead walk bridge, sucking on a straw from a MacDonald's cup. As I round the corner to the stairway there is her mother crouched on the first step, out of sight of the approaching pedestrians. I want to scream at her; "You don't deserve this child!" I fight the urge to grab that poor little baby and run.

I marvel at the little motorbike taxis zipping in and out of traffic with their passenger sitting sidesaddle on the back. Often the passenger is a petite college girl wearing her school uniform consisting of a short, tight, navy skirt with a white blouse; platform sandals, purse slung over one shoulder, cell phone at her ear and at the same time applying lipstick. I have no idea how she keeps her balance on that small back seat.

This month I receive an e-mail from my sister Florence. She writes that her, Laureen and Liz are coming to Thailand for Christmas. I am so excited. This is the best Christmas present imaginable!

Towards the end of October I notice that my room is comfortable without running my fan constantly. Temperatures are still in the high twenties—do you think I am getting used to this heat? This is also Thailand's rainy season and every day rains pour down, sometimes only for short periods, sometimes several hours. October 30 I grab my umbrella and decide to hale a taxi to get to my afternoon class. I walk a block out to the main road and get a taxi immediately. Traffic is backed up and we sit there, not moving an inch. After ten minutes we have still not moved a block so I decide to walk. If I sit here any longer I will be late for class.

I exit the cab, extend my umbrella, and start walking. In three blocks I am wet and my umbrella almost useless. Water is running down the street like a river. My shoes are full of water and squish with each step. I notice other people walking with their shoes in their hands and pant legs rolled up. That is a great idea, I think to myself as I bend down to roll up my pant legs and take off my shoes. Ah, this feels great! Water is half way up my calves and my pant legs keep falling down as I walk—the fabric is so wet it is too heavy to stay up. I am about four or five blocks from class, rain is still pouring down, and I decide to take a short cut. Nope, I still have not learned my lesson! Of course I get lost and end up wandering around the blocks until my directions are mixed up. Finally I make my way back to a main road and continue the long way around arriving at my class twenty minutes late and dripping wet.

I walk into the foyer of this impeccably clean government building and cross the floor to the bathroom leaving a trail of water dripping behind. As I turn to enter the bathroom I see the cleaning lady mopping up behind me. How embarrassing! I take my suit jacket off, slick back my wet hair and proceed to my classroom in bare feet. Five students out of my class of eight are waiting for me. They are surprised to see me and say they did not think I would make it today. I guess this downpour is enough to deter most people.

By November 1 I have been wearing my custom made clothes for a month, and all of a sudden they are too big. Not just a little too big, but *falling off* too big! I call the tailor, reach the owner of the shop, and ask if they will alter them. "Of course," replies Sandy, "alterations are included in the package price." I am thrilled and after I drop them off I stop at a blue jean shop. I pick a size 33 to try on—too big. I cannot believe it! I ask the clerk to bring me a size 32, then a size 31 and then a 30. I am shocked! How did this happen without me even noticing? I have not been on a scale for months and my guess is I have lost twenty pounds or more. It must be the change in diet or maybe the heat melting off the fat. I am ecstatic! This is the weight I should be.

My diet has changed immensely since I have come to Thailand. The heat seems to suppress ones appetite and contribute to drinking much more water. A diet consisting mainly of rice and veggies would also account for some weight loss. Another thing I have noticed is that I very seldom have a beer or other alcoholic drink. This I also attribute to the heat.

I really enjoy teaching my adult classes. Today, November 5, in my afternoon class we have an incident. One of my students, Ing, has fallen in love with his teacher. Unlike most Thai men, he is tall (about 6' 1"), very slim with wavy black hair and deep brown eyes. I estimate his age to be about thirty. Every day he comes into class early and leaves late. He looks at me out of those huge brown eyes with utter adoration. *Oh if I was only twenty years younger.* Today we finish our lessons early and use the remaining time for conversation. My students ask question about Canada, then about me. Am I married, do I have kids?

"Yes I have three kids," I reply.

Tony breaks in and asks in a surprised voice, "How old are you?"

My first thought is, I don't need to tell you that. In that same moment I change my mind. This is my chance to let Ing know that I am probably as old as his mother. So I answer, "Fifty-four." Instantaneously Ing's head drops to the table resting on his folded arms. Now what do I do? I fight the urge to go around the table, put my arms around his shoulders and comfort him, as I would my son. Thankfully the rest of the class continues to ask questions. I am sure they are aware of Ing's pain and are giving him time to compose himself. For five minutes he sits there with his head in his arms then quietly gets up and leaves the room. My heart is breaking for him. Just before we wrap up the class

Ing returns to the room, composed, and takes his seat. From this day forward he stops coming in early and leaving late. He is still an excellent student and never misses a class, but he is different.

November is the month of Loi Krathong Day, or the Festival of Lights—held on the full-moon day of the 12th Thai lunar month, which this year is November 19. This special celebration is probably the most romantic festival in the country. People gather by the waterside in the evening and float handcrafted lotus shaped vessels, made from banana leaves and beautifully decorated with flowers, candles and incense, as a symbol of thanks and worship to the Goddess of Water. The streets are lined with people selling these little vessels so I buy one and take part in the ceremonies. What an amazing evening watching hundreds of flickering candles float down the river.

Time is passing quickly. I am kept busy with classes in different parts of the city. December 5 is the King's 75th birthday and consequently a holiday. I go for a bike ride to Kanchanaburi with Graham, a biker from the USA whom I met through Horizon's Unlimited Web site. He has been living in Thailand for several years and is an avid biker. Graham knows these roads so he leads me on some twisty, mountainous back roads to Kanchanaburi where we stop at the Bridge over river Kwai. The bridge is packed with tourists so we do not bother walking across. Maybe I will come back with my sisters. We take a different route through the hills back to Bangkok—a pleasant ride and such a treat following someone who knows the area.

My adult classes should have been finished before Christmas but with all the Thai holidays they will not finish until January. I talk to Susan about my sisters coming and make sure she does not schedule me for those two weeks. My weekend classes will finish late February and it will be time to move on. I feel ready to resume my traveling. I send an e-mail to the president for Servas Nepal—it will be great if I can make a contact before my arrival in Nepal.

December 26 has finally arrived! I have been counting down the days. I get up early to wash my floor before going to the airport. The pollution in Bangkok is so bad I can wash my floor every day and still have dirty socks by the end of the day. Upon arrival at the airport I find a coffee and wait and watch the electronic arrival board. My excitement mounts as I see SQ062 has landed. It will be at least half an hour before they are through customs. I pace the floor stretching my neck to look over the crowd. Finally I spot them. We hug, and cry, and hold up traffic until one of the taxi vultures tells us to move on. I am so excited I can hardly believe my sisters are here!

We spend the next two days touring the sights of Bangkok. I notice the sweat pouring down the faces of my sisters, dripping off their foreheads into their eyes and the corners of their mouths. Liz looks at me and says, "How come you're not sweating?"

"I guess my body has adjusted somewhat to this heat," I reply with a chuckle. "It was worse than this when I first arrived. I came in their hottest season."

They cannot imagine it being hotter than this. I tell them a story about one of my adult students coming to class last week in a bulky turtleneck sweater. This is winter weather for the local people. Temperatures are in the mid to high twenties.

In two days we tour the Grande Palace, take a long-tail boat ride up the river, visit the reclining Buddha, have a foot massage, shop in the markets at Panthip Plaza, ride the bus and the sky train, packing in as much as we can before picking up our rental car and heading north. Our road trip north takes us through the ruins of Ayutthaya, which was the capital city of Thailand from 1350 to 1776, and the ruins of Sukhothai, which was the first capital city of the Kingdom of Thailand prior to 1350.

We continue north on highway 101 then 11 through the mountains to Chiang Mai. The roads twist up and down winding through the mountains and I cannot help but think how much fun this would be on my bike. The trees are green, the sky is blue and the sun is shining—what a glorious day!

December 31 we arrive in Chiang Mai about noon and make our way to the centre of the old city, which is surrounded by a moat and a high cement wall. The wall is now crumbling and only partially remains but one still gets a sense of protection. We have no reservations so our first task is to find a room. We find a great hotel named *Top Notch Hotel*—two levels of rooms built around an open courtyard containing a large swimming pool, gardens and restaurant for five hundred baht a night. We are able to book two rooms on the second level overlooking the pool. What a great deal! We wander around the old city then find an outdoor restaurant for New Years Eve dinner. The evening is warm and we all agree this is better than the cold winters in Canada. A live band entertains us all evening until almost midnight when we return to our hotel to watch the fireworks from our balcony. A fabulous ending to another year!

January 1, 2003, begins a whole new year. I have been away from home seventeen months and am so thankful to have this short time with my sisters. My thoughts go to my sister Irene and I wish she were here too.

Today we have booked an adventure tour. We are part of a group of ten packed tightly into a van with our tour guide, his daughter and the driver. Our first stop is about half an hour away where we mount the elephants that take us farther up the mountains. Two people sit on a bench-like saddle strapped to the back of the elephant while the trainer sits on his head. Liz and I are like two kids again and are first in line for the ride. Laureen is terrified so her and Florence wait until last to load. The elephants cross the river then begin their climb up the mountain through the jungle. The ride is smooth—these huge animals are very sure-footed. After about an hour we dismount and begin our trek through the jungle to the Hmong Hill Tribe village, Thailand's second largest hill tribe. There are about twenty-five families in this tribe. They speak their own dialect and do not speak or understand Thai. About fifteen families are Animism (they believe in spirits), five families are Buddhist and five families are Christian—they all live together peacefully. These hill tribe people originate from southern China. Their huts have no windows, only one door. They fear the bad spirits will come in the windows and make their children sick. The children do not attend school. There is no teacher who speaks both Thai and their dialect; besides it is difficult to find a teacher who wants to live that far into the mountains away from the conveniences of town. They grow all there own food; raise a few pigs and travel on foot.

From here we trek out to the road crossing the river on a long swinging bridge with a deck made of bamboo, and less than a meter wide. We hold on to the guide ropes on each side about sixty centimeters above the deck. The bridge is a tad shaky! We hike past banana trees in bloom and loaded with racks of bananas, lush forest of multi-colored green, papayas hanging from trees—there is just no end to the beauty. When we reach the road we all pile into the van and are driven to a local restaurant in the mountains where a meal has been prepared just for our group. The food is delicious and plentiful—we are fed well.

Our day is only half over. From lunch we trek up to one of the Karen Hill Tribe villages. This is only one of four Karen Tribes and amongst them they make up the largest of the hill tribe groups in Thailand. As we near the village, children come running down the hill with beads and ornaments in their hands. Each of them presses to sell their trinkets. The Karen hill tribe originated from Myanmar, formerly known as Burma. Their beliefs range from animism, Buddhism to Christianity. Single women wear white and a man can obtain a wife by offering a pig. Women weave brightly colored blankets and scarves and sell them to the tourists that visit.

From here we stop at some picturesque waterfalls before going river rafting. The rafts are each made with eight or nine hollow bamboo logs, about ten to fifteen centimeters in diameter and six to seven meters long, strapped together in about four places with a skinny bamboo log placed perpendicular across the long logs. All four of us board one raft and are instructed to sit close together near the centre. Our captain is a short but sturdy young Thai man named Jang, who will maneuver our raft down the river. "If we too heavy, raft go like submarine—submarine no fun," Jang says very seriously. We all laugh. Jang carries a long pole, about four times his height, which he uses to shove into the water or against the banks to maneuver the raft around corners and rocks, over rapids, and to avoid other rafts. We get a little wet now and again but have a great time. Jang is very skilled at his craft and takes us safely on an exciting ride down the river.

Florence and Laureen are sick throughout the night. They were out of bottled water so drank tap water to swallow their vitamins. I apologize for laughing but the situation is quite ironic—definitely worth a chuckle. The good news is they only lost one day.

Liz and I go in search of a Laundromat and encounter a truck being pulled out of the moat. While we stand and watch we are befriended by a handsome Thai man who tells us what happened. "There were five tourists in the truck. I run, run, run and jump in the water—kick, kick, kick to break the window—gulp, gulp, gulp, drink too much water—can't hold onto them and must go up," he says with a comical flourish of actions and excitement. We try hard, and with difficulty, to keep a serious face. He continues on saying, "One other passenger dives in and helps two elderly people to safety. All passengers were rescued."

As we turn to leave this man introduces himself as Cha and asks if we would like to take a tour. Cha is an independent tour operator who walks the streets soliciting business. We hesitate at first but when he introduces us to his wife we relax and decide to take the tour. We visit the butterfly and orchid farm, then the snake farm (pythons, cobras, water snakes) where Liz holds a python around her neck. Not me, no amount of coaxing is going to get me to snuggle with a snake! Next stop is the monkey farm—Liz participates in the show again. She is having a great time. Some of these monkeys are trained to pick coconuts during harvest. From here we go to the silk factory. Silk comes from the oval cocoon around the silk worm. The silk worm feeds on Mulberry leaves then forms a cocoon about three to five centimeters long and two to three centimeters wide. The color is bright yellow and if you shake it you can hear the worm rattle inside. If left to hatch it becomes a moth. To get the thread out, the cocoon must be boiled before the silk-worm hatches. One cocoon makes five hundred meters of silk thread. Last stop for the day is the gem gallery. This business has their marketing strategy fine-tuned. We enter in a long gallery area where we are offered a drink—pop, juice, water, coffee, tea, beer, wine or a cocktail. How is that to loosen up your customers? Then we are each assigned a sales clerk who follows us around the huge showroom and opens each showcase that we show an interest in. When customers have to wait for anything, such as ring sizing, they are ushered into the lounge and offered more cocktails. My guess is they do a whopping business.

Cha and Mian are wonderful hosts and tour guides. Mian tells me she was fifteen when she married Cha and that many Thai girls still marry at ages thirteen to fifteen. "European men," she says, "come to Thailand and pick up eleven to fifteen year old girls." She talks to her daughter about the dangers and traps young girls get caught in. Her wish is to see her daughter finish school and go to university. This is a common goal of parents around the world—it is what we all wish for.

January 3 we leave Chiang Mai taking in the splendid mountain scenery, visiting more historical sites over the next two days, then stopping for a day at the beach on the Gulf of Thailand before returning to Bangkok on January 5. Only two days before the girls fly back to Canada. We decide to go shopping at a huge night market, highly recommended by tourists and locals alike. From my apartment we take the elevator down four floors. The elevator stops on level three and a petite, Thai lady steps in. Instantly the alarm goes off and she bolts out the door, turns and looks at us with huge eyes and a shocked look on her face. I can almost see her counting, 1, 2, 3, 4. The elevator door closes and we burst out laughing. Near the controls there is a sign stating; *Maximum capacity six people.* That must mean six Thai people—not Canadians.

January 7 we are up early and say our goodbyes. I am sad to see them leave. My thoughts at this moment are to *get on with my journey and complete my goal to travel around the world so I can return to my family.* My sisters take a taxi to the airport and I ride my motorcycle to work. These next two weeks wrap up my adult classes and I start to make plans to move on. My weekend classes finish near the end of February so I will plan on leaving the first week of March. I also have to make one more exit out of Thailand to renew my visa and get a valid white paper for my motorcycle. I am sure the photocopy paper the officials stamped at the border coming back from Cambodia will not be acceptable at the freight forwarders.

January 14 is my last day of adult classes. I cannot express how much I have enjoyed meeting and teaching these people. They have made my experience in teaching English as a foreign language one I will cherish forever. I am presented with several little gifts but the best gift of all is from Wut. He stands and gives a short speech on behalf of the class thanking me for the way I communicated with them and for helping them to feel comfortable. Then they give a big applaud. Yes, I will miss them all.

Now that my only teaching commitment is on the weekends and completing reports for the adult classes, I spend time making plans and getting organized to fly to Nepal early in March. I call a few shipping companies and it looks like I will use Hellman's Logistics again. They quote me thirty thousand baht to fly my bike to Katmandu, Nepal. That is not too bad, but my own flight will be less than eight thousand. Hardly seems reasonable.

I make a trip to the Laos Embassy to get a visa for a short trip to Laos. When I reach the gates of the Embassy the guard instructs me to shut my bike off and push it into the parking lot. The cost for a Laos visa is approximately sixty-two dollars Canadian—much more than I expected. They have given me sixty days, which is way more than I need since I only plan on going for a week. During my wait here I chat with two ladies from British Columbia who are also going to Laos. They appear to be well traveled. It would be neat if we met up somewhere in Laos. I return to my bike and as soon as I sit on it the guard appears at my side and tells me to push the bike out of the gates before I start it. So I graciously comply and stop at the very edge of the gate and fire it up. Oh … I am feeling so … nasty.

From here I ride to the Thai Embassy to request a one or two day extension on my Thai visa. It will expire before I get to the Laos border. The gal at the wicket is very helpful and tells me there is no penalty if I am only one day over. Wow, that helps.

Now I have another dilemma facing me. The registration for my bike expires and the Canadian regulations prevent me from getting it renewed through the mail, by phone, by e-mail, by my sister or even with the assistance of the Canadian Consulate. I must present my registration in person and my bike has to be there also. Well now, am I really going to fly my bike and myself home to do that? I don't think so! I do some investigating through the Internet with other world travelers and conclude that, in fact, I cannot get my registration renewed legally while out of the country. Now what do I do? I will have to follow the advice of fellow riders …

Chapter 11

Laos

January 27, 2003, I am on my way to the Laos border. At the Thai border I get my passport stamped and am charged a penalty of two hundred baht for being one day over. I argue with the clerk telling him that the Embassy in Bangkok said there is no penalty for being one day over. He simply says, "That's in Bangkok, not here." Go figure! One of the officers escorts me across two lanes of traffic to the office where I must pay my fine before continuing. Back at the bike, as I am putting on my helmet, I begin to think they are not going to ask for the white paper, but before I can get my helmet on a second officer comes over and points me to another line. I take my bike papers and passport to the wicket and wait. The officer studies my photo copied paper and questions it. I explain the situation about entering Thailand from Cambodia, but he is not accepting my story. For several minutes we discuss the issue and by now there is a line forming behind me. I turn to the man behind me and apologize for the delay. I can tell the clerk in his little booth is becoming agitated, not knowing what to do. He continues to tell me, "The white paper is no good!" I continue to tell him that the Thai officials at the Cambodia border assured me this paper *is* good. I'm not leaving until this paper is stamped. I turn a second time and apologize to the people in line behind me. Finally the officer stamps the paper and waves me aside as if to say, "Get out of here." Whew—what a relief!

Now I can ride across the Friendship Bridge to Laos. The bridge crosses over the Mekong River connecting Nong Khai, Thailand to Vientiane, Laos—and the two border crossings. The bridge is 1,170 meters long, has two 3.5-meter wide lanes for vehicle traffic, two 1.5-meter wide footpaths and an unfinished single railway line in the middle. Officials have just recently allowed motorcycles to cross this bridge. As I reach the Lao end of the bridge there are traffic lights indicating the change over from left lane to right. Traffic drives on the right in Laos.

In no time at all I am at the Lao border gates. It takes two hours to clear customs before being directed to the booth where an officer stamps my visa and staples in a departure card. Next I am directed to room eight in the customs building where I must request a vehicle permit. I enter the room, which is occupied by two men. After a few questions they send me to room six, where I am met by a little man with a squeaky little voice. Now begins the second round of the *game of twenty questions.* He goes over all the regulations with me before he finally signs the paper and says, in his annoying squeaky voice, "I am giving you fifteen days—you cannot leave the Province of Viang Chan. If you want this extended you must go to the Embassy of Communication in Vientiane. Take this document to room five."

Off I go to room five, where a young lady records the information. She fills out the document and records it manually in a huge ledger. She is very pleasant and quite in awe that I am traveling alone *and* by motorcycle. A second girl sits at a desk at the side of the room—doing nothing as far as I can determine. Once the document is filled out she is sent to get it photocopied. I guess that is what her job is. I pay ten baht for this service. Money paid, I am told to return to room eight where a different man tells me I have seven days on this carnet. I argue that Mr. Squeaky Voice said I would have fifteen days. This is really beginning to annoy me! Maybe these old men think they can intimidate me because I'm female or, maybe this is one of those times I should offer a bribe. With my seven-day carnet I am sent back to the customs booth to get the document stamped. The cost is two hundred and forty baht and another ten minutes while Mr. Typist plucks away with one finger entering the data. Now I think I am done ... but ... oh no, what's this? One more officer has to stamp the carnet ... another officer has to check it and take his copy ... *Finally I am Free!* I ride through the gates to the insurance office just fifty meters away to buy bike insurance. Mr. Squeaky Voice had made a point of telling me my Thai Insurance is "no good here," and I am sure he is watching to make sure I stop. The insurance agent is very pleasant but by this time, after three hours of being shuffled back and forth, I am so annoyed with the border crossing system that I cannot even give him a smile. The cost of insurance is approximately one dollar a day.

At last I am on my way to Vientiane, I ride through construction at the border on to a roughly paved two lane highway with no lines and countless pavement patches, bumps, dips and holes. Driving is on the right in vehicles with steering wheels on the left. I almost feel like I am back home. In Vientiane I stop at a bank to change some money. The currency is the Kip and one Canadian dollar is equal to 5,169.21 kip, or 165 baht equals 41,000 kip. They only exchange US dollars and baht, so I exchange some of my baht for kip.

When I return to my bike, a street cop approaches. He asks to see my license and tells me I cannot park here. I look around for signs and do not see any but hand over my license and carnet. He continues to say you cannot park here and I reply, "I understand, I'm moving." A second cop arrives on the scene and asks if I need help. Cop One repeats his statement a couple more times and finally I get the picture—he wants money! This has not been a good day of encounters with authoritative figures and I am fed up. I throw up my hands and say, "Fine, write me a ticket." All of a sudden Cop One becomes very pleasant. He folds my carnet around my license and hands it back to me. I ask for directions to Saylomyen Guesthouse. Now Cop One wants to show off to his buddies and is very helpful giving me directions.

The afternoon is still early so once I check into the guesthouse I unpack, shower and go exploring. Vientiane is a city of French influence, which is obvious in much of the architectural design. There is quite a mixture of old and new architecture in this growing city. I walk to the Patuxai (Victory Monument), a monument that is reminiscent of the Arc de Triomphe in Paris—a huge cement arch built in 1962 with cement purchased from the USA. The monument is to commemorate the Lao who died in pre-revolutionary wars. From here I walk to Pha That Luang, The Great Sacred Stupa. It is the most important national monument and religious symbol in Laos. Built by King Settathirat in 1566, it stands forty-five meters high and is surrounded by a high walled cloister with tiny windows.

Fascinating structures—but that is enough walking for one day. It's time to find one of the many French bakeries in town and indulge in some pastries.

Next morning I am up early to ride higher into the mountains. Laos is seventy percent mountains and plateaus, and fifty percent forest. I take highway 13 going north towards Vang Vieng, a favorite spot for backpackers. This is not a highway where one can make good progress; it is dotted with towns and villages every few kilometers. As I ride higher into the mountains the villages become smaller and less urbanized. Bamboo huts line the highway both on the cliff side and the hillside—often on a curve edging it's way around the mountain.

As I climb higher I realize there are no vehicles in many of the villages, I have the road pretty much to myself. I pass people, young and old, walking along the road carrying wood and grain bundles on their back. Some people are stationed along the road gathering, spreading or pounding sheaves of grain. Women and girls are clad in long wrap around skirts and blouses—no blue jeans here to work in. Even the very young children have their duty to perform. On their feet they wear sandals or flip-flops. In many of the villages high in the mountains it does not appear that the children attend school. I am passing through on weekdays when children should be in school but here they are playing or working along the side of the road. As I ride slowly through the villages I notice the withered, elderly grandparents sitting on benches or chairs at the fronts of the buildings watching the young children run and play amongst the huts that dangle off the side of the cliff. I wonder if a child has ever fallen over the cliff. In our protective society we would be building high fences to protect us from ourselves.

I pass a lean-to shelter where men are gathered around laughing and visiting. It seems the women and children do most of the work here. Women and very young girls and boys trudge up the mountain roads with large bundles of wood or sheaves of grain strapped to their backs. Children look to be five to ten years of age, gathering stocks of grain and spreading it along the side of the road to dry or pounding the sheaves on the pavement. I think of my little grandchildren at home and my heart aches to see these children working instead of going to school.

The mountain road is quite smooth with the exception of many of the curves where the pavement has given out to dirt, gravel and potholes. I keep a keen eye out for animals on the road, not wild ones, but village animals—chickens, geese, ducks and turkeys, dogs, pigs, goats and cows roaming the highway. As I round a curve coming into a small village I am met by a flock of chickens. They scatter in all directions in front of me; I feel a *bump* and looking back in my rear view mirror see a pretty colored hen lying on the road. I really want to stop and take it to its owner but am afraid of what they might do to me, so I keep riding.

On one stretch of the highway I encounter army troops with their rifles resting against their shoulders. They wave me through and I am shocked at how young these men are. To me they appear to be young teenage boys and I wonder how responsible they are with their rifles. A little farther down the road I see another group of young men clad in army gear sitting and lying in the shade at the side of the road. I wonder what their purpose is but can only guess, so I tell myself they are here for emergency situations.

About noon I reach Phou Khoun and stop for food and water. The streets are dusty and packed with people, carts, bikes, big trucks and a couple of pick up trucks. I park my bike where I can see it from anywhere in the block and head for an open front restaurant. I just get seated when a white male about my age joins me.

He introduces himself as Joe, from Guelph, Ontario. He is cycling this mountain road all the way to Luang Prabang. "The next stretch will be the most difficult," he says. "The road climbs more steeply up the mountain until you reach Luang Prabang." I am glad to be on a motorcycle and not pedaling. As we chat, Joe tells me I have already passed Vang Vieng. The town is off the main highway and I did not see any signs, so rode right past. Meeting someone from your own country when you are so far from home is exciting. It gives you a certain feeling of camaraderie.

Phou Khoun is the intersection where the road goes east to Phonsavan (Plain of Jars) or north to Luang Prabang, in the province of Louangphrabang. Since I have missed Vang Vieng I decide to continue north—oops, I'm not supposed to leave Viang Chan province.

The city of Luang Prabang is located on the Mekong River about 425 kilometers north of Vientiane. Until the communist takeover in 1975, it was the Royal Capital of the Kingdom of Laos. In 1995 it was listed as a UNESCO World Heritage site and I really don't want to miss it since I am so close—only one hundred and thirty kilometers away. I decide to take my chances and leave the province of Viang Chan.

I arrive in Luang Prabang about 5:00 PM and find a great guesthouse for seventy-five thousand kip (eleven dollars Canadian). I search out the market for something to eat before it gets too dark and cannot resist a stroll through the stalls packed with locally made crafts, ornamental Buddhas, clothes and much, much more.

When I return to the guesthouse and unload my bike I find that my water bottle has leaked and all my stamped papers from the border are wet. I peel each sheet of paper apart carefully and spread them on the floor of my room to dry. The red stamp on the Laos carnet is nothing more than a red blotch. I wonder what problems that will create when I return to the border. Oh well, no point in worrying about that now.

Time only allows me one day to see as much of Luang Prabang as I can. It does not take long to realize it would take a few weeks to really explore the area. In this one short day I climb the hill of Wats and witness a fabulous view of Luang Prabang, the Mekong River and surrounding mountains, visit the Royal Theatre and the Former Royal Palace. There are caves to explore, hiking trails to take and so much more to discover. I will just have to come back another day.

On my return ride to Vientiane I find Vang Vieng about half way between Luang Prabang and Vientiane. This town is very popular with backpackers and has several new guesthouses, Internet cafes, and restaurants. The attraction here is trekking and caving, which I cannot indulge in at this time. I pick a comfortable looking guesthouse and wander through the streets that seem to come alive in the evening once the backpackers return from their day treks.

Laos is a beautiful country where one can escape the stress of modern day life and experience the tranquility of a world dominated by Buddhism. It is a country just waiting to be explored.

On the afternoon of January 30 I cross the border back to Thailand. At the Laos border I am sent hither and yon before finally getting an officer to stamp out my carnet. I am lucky to get a customs officer who is pleasant and chuckles when he sees the water stained, smudged, red blotch for an entrance stamp on my carnet. He stamps it out and gives me a huge smile. I cross the Friendship Bridge a second time and stop at the Thailand border. All goes smoothly this time and I am issued a legitimate carnet for my bike. This is very important because I need this document to ship my bike to Nepal. The shipping agent was very clear on that point—they would not ship my bike without an official carnet issued by the Thai authorities.

Only one week after I return from Laos there is an ambush six kilometers north of Vang Vieng. Ten people were killed—two foreigners and eight Lao. I have not been able to find out any more than the small article printed in the Bangkok Post. I keep asking but no one knows. It is almost like it never happened or it is of little significance. Pretty scary considering I was just on that road!

Chapter 12

Thailand, Part III

Once through customs I take highway 211 following the Mekong River west and north in Thailand. For several kilometers the Mighty Mekong divides Thailand and Laos. The scenery is spectacular here and I stop at a little park in Sang Khom to take some pictures along the river. There are six men leaning against the cement guardrail overlooking the river when I ride in. I stop the bike and dig out my camera remaining aware of my surroundings. When I look up one of the men is approaching me and looks very intently at my bike while another man pulls out a walkie-talkie and begins talking to someone. Before I have time to take two pictures, four more men arrive in a truck. They are way too interested in my bike and my instincts tell me to get out of here! As I put on my helmet and gloves two men approach from the right, I can sense someone behind me and two men on my left are walking towards the park entrance. I quickly get on the bike and turn the key. The first man steps in front of my bike and asks, "Are you from America? How much?" as he waves towards the bike.

"I'm from Canada," I reply.

"How much US dollars?" he asks.

I think for a moment wondering what I should say … "Six thousand US" I reply.

He says "okay" and steps to the left peering at the bike. I crank the throttle and take off as quickly as I can, feeling somewhat shaken. It feels like a scene from a movie where the thugs move in from all directions for the attack. I watch my rear view mirror closely for the rest of the day and ride farther than I intended, just to put distance between Sang Khom and myself.

The mountain roads and scenery are marvelous. The air is fresh and traffic is minimal. I take highway 201 to Loei then 203 to Phu Rua and ride until I see a B&B sign. I find a wonderful little chalet for four hundred baht, big enough to sleep five people and with its own little yard. I wish my sisters were here now—they would love this. It is so peaceful and pretty. This would be the place to go for a quiet retreat to escape the pollution and noise of Bangkok.

February is a busy month. I finish up my weekend classes, have my bike serviced and new tires installed. The mechanic, Yut, who comes highly recommended by other bikers, says my chain and sprocket are good. For a complete service job and two new tires my bill is 260 dollars Canadian. Great deal! I make arrangements to crate and ship my bike, wash my riding gear and get everything in order to go. I do some last minute sightseeing in and out of Bangkok, update my Web site and submit an article to Horizons Unlimited Web site. I go for *very long* walks every day to get in shape for trekking in Nepal. I load my backpack with books and walk the streets taking the stairways up and down over the busy roads to strengthen my climbing muscles. I am thinking of doing a two or three-week hike in the Himalayas.

February 14 the merchants and street vendors are promoting their products for Valentine's Day. The sidewalks are lined with vendors selling long stemmed roses, flower arrangements, chocolates and many other sweetheart products. There should be no excuse for not having a gift for your loved one. I pass dozens of people with flowers in their hands, heading off to meet that special someone. As for me ... I buy my plane ticket to Nepal today—7,730 baht. I will fly Royal Nepal Air on March 3 at 14:15.

On February 18 I ride my bike to Hellman's Logistics to drop it off for crating and shipping. I am close to Sukumvit 19, the street I would turn right on, when I am stopped by a police check giving out tickets to motorcyclists. Remember traffic drives on the left and motorbikes are supposed to stay in the far left lane with buses, taxis and tuk-tuks pulling in and out. I explain to the officer that I just moved over to the right lane because I have to turn right at Sukumvit 19. He mumbles something about 'thirty meters before the turn' and turns to another officer and says, "Write her a ticket." I end up paying the second officer a bribe of three hundred and ten baht, then ask where Sukumvit 19 is. He pretends not to understand me so I ask a man standing on the sidewalk watching this performance and he tells me the street is just up ahead. I continue on and sure enough, less than fifty meters is my turn for Sukumvit 19. Thailand is definitely not biker friendly—or maybe the system is just so corrupt that officers make it a practice to put extra money in their pockets.

I arrive at Hellman's and, after completing the paperwork with Mr. Tan, disassemble my bike. This always attracts attention. Two gentlemen from the warehouse watch as I remove the windshield, mirrors and top trunk, disconnect and tape the battery cables and drain the fuel. The two men find a container and help drain the fuel then hand the container to me. I ask them if they want to pour the fuel into one of their bikes, which produces big smiles and many thanks. Job complete … once again I have to walk away from my travel companion with much reservation, and hope we will meet again in Nepal.

Possibly it is this anxiety that makes me do what I do next. I walk to MK (Maboondrong) Center, in the heart of Bangkok's big shopping complexes, and have my eyelids (eyeliner) tattooed! Can you believe it? I am terrified as I sit in the chair—it hurts but I tough it out. When the procedure is complete and I look in the mirror I am horrified! The lines are way too black! I look like a raccoon! The tattoo artist assures me that in five days it will be fifty percent lighter. Do I dare believe her?

I decide to walk home. It is a long walk but I do not want to be on the crowded sky train and have people staring at me. On the way I stop in a store and buy eye drops and Q-tips. For the next week I use this to wash the tattoo lines in hopes of lightening them. I am experiencing panic attacks and have to do some deep breathing to calm myself down. I call my daughter Carey and tell her what I have done and that I have ruined my life. She says, "It's okay Mom, you're still beautiful inside. That's what counts." She is so precious. How did I deserve such a wonderful daughter?

Two days later I have a good cry. I am feeling homesick and awful about my eyes, although they are looking much better already. I can now believe the tattoo artist telling me they will lighten by fifty percent. The cry makes me feel much better—I will survive.

On February 24 I send a parcel containing my journals, backup pictures and anything else of importance, home to Carey. It will not be difficult to give away all the stuff I have accumulated for my apartment. In fact, it will feel good.

I do a trial pack of my bike rolls and know I will have to lighten my load considerably before I leave. Mr. Tan calls to tell me it will cost six thousand baht to crate my bike. I almost explode in his ear. He finally agrees to negotiate with the crating company and calls me back later to say they agreed upon four thousand. I am just sure the Thai people love to take advantage of foreigners. Two days later he calls me to say the weight of the shipment is 650 kilograms. Once again I explode in his ear! "How can that be?" I ask. "The weight was 350kgs when I shipped it from Canada and 398kgs when I shipped it from Australia. How can it possibly be 650kgs now? The bike only weighs 250kgs." I am a little frustrated to say the least.

I talk to Khun Tairak about my predicament and he offers to intervene for me. I am so grateful. With his help we manage to get the crate downsized in volume to 450kgs. I have to pay another thousand baht for the re-crating but it will bring the shipping cost down considerably. In total it cost me five thousand baht for crating and thirty-five thousand, eight hundred for shipping—approximately $1550 Canadian, complete.

March 1 and 2, Saturday and Sunday, are report card days for my weekend classes. The children are excited to receive their diplomas for completing their class. Most of them will enroll again for the next level of English. Many parents attend this important day and one Mom asks me if I will be teaching the next term. When I tell her that I am leaving she says, "Oh no, we really like you."

I am honoured and cannot think of a better way to complete my teaching experience.

Some interesting current events about Thailand:

- The death penalty is facing a firing squad. The Government has just passed a policy to put away machine guns. Death is now by lethal injection. Lobbyists are protesting—pushing to abolish the death penalty.

- Health insurance is Government funded and available to everyone.

- Their pollution problem is so big they don't know *where to begin* to fix it.

- Thai people are very loyal to their King and Queen.

- Most Thai students do not work while they attend college. They are expected to focus totally on their studies.

I have had a great experience in Thailand. The police system is totally corrupt. Some say the reason is because their pay is so low they rely on bribes to make a decent living. I realize that one must stay more than two or three weeks to really know what the culture is like. I have been here eight months—long enough. I am ready to move on.

Monday, March 4, 2003, I fly to Nepal.

Preview

Untamed Spirit II — Living a Dream

I have been away from home for nineteen months and only traveled half way around the world. Book II; *Untamed Spirit II, Living a Dream* continues my journey beginning in Nepal, then on to Tibet, India, Pakistan, Iran, Turkey, Europe, Morocco, South America, Central America, Mexico, USA and home to Canada.

In Kathmandu, Nepal I am faced with challenges of horrendous pollution and my first accident. The accident leaves me shaken but I do not let that stop me. There is much to see and do here and one of my dreams is to hike in the Himalayan Mountains. Another passion is to visit the Potala Palace in Lhasa, in the lost country of Tibet. This may be my only visit here so I must make the most of it.

It is April 2003 when I cross the border into Bahar, the poorest state in India. Here I'm met with a whole new set of challenges as I travel through the northern states. Temperatures are already climbing into the high thirties making my riding gear unbearably hot and uncomfortable. The heat intensifies as I travel west into Pakistan and Iran. Some of my most memorable experiences come from these two countries. One such experience is celebrating my 55th birthday with police officers and hotel staff in D.G. Khan, Pakistan, and then continuing on with a police escort for the day.

I take my time traveling through Turkey and still only see a small part of it. The history here is fascinating. There is no better education than travel. The price of fuel jumps dramatically—around $2.00 per liter. Europe is extremely expensive. One Euro is approximately $1.60 Canadian, so I travel quickly through Greece, Italy, Slovenia, Austria, Czech Republic, Poland, Lithuania, Sweden, Norway, Denmark and Germany. I spend more time in The Netherlands visiting with fellow bikers I met on the road in Malaysia. In France I am fortunate to stay with a lady I met at a hostel in Italy, giving me time to explore Paris. Spain captures my heart leaving me yearning to go back.

New Years 2004 finds me in Rabat, Morocco. Unfortunately Morocco is the only country in Africa that I visit. My experience here is un-nerving at times and I'm happy to return to Spain where I ship my bike on to South America. I arrive in Buenos Aires on January 28 and begin planning my route through Argentina, Chile, Bolivia, Peru and Ecuador. Another rider from Edmonton, Alberta joins me in Chile and we ride together through South and Central America all the way to Guatemala. I welcome the companionship, but riding with another person presents a whole new set of challenges.

I have been on this journey for almost three years and am anxious to get home. My riding companion and I part ways in Guatemala and I continue through Mexico, alone once again. By June 30th I arrive back in Edmonton, happy to be home. It has been an amazing adventure and an education of a lifetime.

Read about my exciting adventures on the second half of my journey in **Untamed Spirit II—Living a Dream**.

ABOUT THE AUTHOR

DORIS MARON was born June 5, 1948, the seventh child in a family of nine. At an early age she dreamed of traveling to other parts of the world. Her passion to experience all that life has to offer took her into several career changes and many adventures before she embraced her love to travel. From her travel journals she now writes and shares her adventures with the world.

be obtained at www.ICGtesting.com

0B/855/P

CPSIA information c
Printed in the USA
LVOW080548100713

342073LV000